CONSIDERATIONS ON PAINTING

Library of American Art

CONSIDERATIONS ON PAINTING

Lectures Given in the Year 1893 at the
Metropolitan Museum of Art

By John La Farge

Kennedy Galleries, Inc. • *Da Capo Press*
New York • *1969*

This edition of *Considerations on Painting* is an unabridged republication of the first edition published in New York and London in 1895.

Library of Congress Catalog Card Number 70-96111

Published by
Kennedy Galleries, Inc.
20 East 56th Street, New York, N.Y. 10022

and

Da Capo Press
A Division of Plenum Publishing Corporation
227 West 17th Street, New York, N.Y. 10011

CONSIDERATIONS ON PAINTING

CONSIDERATIONS ON PAINTING

LECTURES
GIVEN IN THE YEAR 1893
AT THE METROPOLITAN MUSEUM
OF NEW YORK

BY

JOHN LA FARGE

New York
MACMILLAN AND CO.
AND LONDON
1895

Norwood Press
J. S. Cushing & Co. — Berwick & Smith
Norwood Mass. U.S.A.

PREFACE.

I FEEL that the printing of my lectures brings with it a certain difficulty. Lectures intended to be read within the Museum, with a continual reference, implied and often expressed, to the place, the objects gathered within it and their associations, must have had a certain fitness which will be more or less diminished when they come to be read under different conditions. Moreover, they were written and spoken with an idea always present in my mind: that I had a class of students whom I was addressing, and that my other auditors stood in a more remote relation to me. Certain appeals to my teaching, certain allusions to the practice of the students and to their position of relative dependence and inferiority of age or acquaintance with the world, of little or no significance to my readers, are thus explained.

I have not seen any way of so modifying these lectures as to suit my feelings and wishes in the present; nor could I have found the time to do so had I seen my way clearly to that end. Even the time that I gave to their preparation for the Museum course had to be taken out of the hours of personal teaching; and they bear the mark of a more temporary consideration on my part than would suit me had I from the first thought of publishing them.

At the same time, there is always something in work done for a special practical purpose which through its very contexture makes a practical answer to many questions; and I have hoped that with some slight modifications and explanations I may manage to make my readers feel that these lectures are for them. I need not add, I think, that there is little in these pages that pretends to be novel. Indeed, I should like to appeal to the memories stored in the consciousness of my readers, and ask if their own observation does not bear me out in mine.

J. L. F.

PARIS, 1895.

LECTURE I

ESSENTIAL DIVISIONS OF THE WORK OF ART

SYNOPSIS OF LECTURE I.

Proposed plan of the lectures. — Consideration of what museums of art offer for study. — Classification of the kinds of lessons to be derived from their contents. — Difference between such a course of study and the usual practical studies which must have preceded. — Why more specially painting and sculpture are called art. — The artist expresses what is in reality himself. — Personality impossible to conceal in the work of art. — The thought that makes the work of art not reflection or reflective thought. — Deficiencies of the thought which analyzes; genius as the power of co-ordinating innumerable memories. — The record of memories even in the superficial appearance of the work of art. — Many essential characteristics inseparable from the work of art must be lost to us in certain cases. — Style is living form. — Certain forms consequently impossible to imitate. — Ruysdael and Millet. — What happens when methods are separated from sentiment. — What happens to imitators. — Loss of the meaning and influence of the work of art when it has been made to appeal especially to momentary interests. — Rules exist for art, not art for rules. — But art is a language and has a grammar which varies only as language varies. — Preparation of the artist for the free world that he creates. — We help him to make it: and taste may be a form of genius. — Possibility of living in the work of others. — In what true originality consists. — What we learn to know is men.

2

LECTURE I.

ESSENTIAL DIVISIONS OF THE WORK OF ART.

It is my intention, in the lectures which I begin to-day, to supplement and to accentuate, in a more fixed and reasoned form, the teachings which I give to my students in a practical way. Whether they be written out in literary shape, or abandoned to the chance form of an ordinary talk, they will be meant to explain the philosophy of usual teaching. Sometimes what I shall have to say may seem rather formal, somewhat abstract, perhaps thereby a little tiresome. At other times I shall be forced into details which are best given in the least conventional manner; and thereby I may seem to be stepping down from a high plane. But these difficulties are inherent in the nature of the case, and in the unaccustomed position which the

3

artist takes when he attempts to give explanations in words of what he thinks without words.

I shall begin by some reference to the differences between such a course of study as this one which we have undertaken in connection with the collections of a museum, and the usual practical studies which must have preceded ours.

I should then like to consider what museums of art offer for study, and to analyze and classify the kinds of lessons to be derived from their contents;

Also to consider how the artist has expressed his view of the world, how he has seen it, with what body and senses, what hereditary memories, what memories of acquired liking, what development of memory through study, and what personal combination of all these factors;

To consider next how museums are collections of works by such men of all periods, who fully made use of all these means; how they contain, moreover, things left by imitators of such works, who only used part of these means of memory.

In such an analysis I should try to explain

what the principles of these studies might be. These various considerations I shall repeat in different ways, from different points of view; more especially in these lectures at the beginning.

I also propose to inquire as to the way in which things that interest us through sight are seen, and what is our sight, and how we use it in the art of painting. And perhaps, if there be time, I may call the attention of my students to what painters and other artists have said about their arts, and connect these statements with our studies. The difficulty for the artist who works in things to put his thoughts into words is a natural difficulty, and much of what we shall study together will make the causes of it evident. All efforts made in any direction are made at the expense of our being able equally well to carry out others of a different kind; the artist's nature has warned him of the loss, and his usual willingness to be satisfied without words is not misplaced.

What I shall have to say to you will be addressed more especially to my students, whether or not I may have repeated these points, their derivations and conclusions, to them, during the course of lessons, or whether I have merely implied them.

I have come into addressing you upon these matters through having been chosen by the Museum to help, by organized study, in securing an extension and a more certain result of the advantages offered to every one in its collections. This choice might as well have fallen upon one of many other artists, and all that I can hope is that I may be able to do as well as any of the others of whom I think.

The methods of teaching used in schools, — which, taking a pupil as he may be found, begin with him, if necessary, at the beginning, place unknown tools in his hands, teach him quite as much the use of his body (of his hands, I mean, and his eyes) as of his mind, prepare him gradually to know that there is a language that he can speak, teach him its average alphabet, its average spelling, its average grammar, — these methods which are meant for the child have limitations unsuitable to an older and better informed stage of mind. In the first place, any form of obedience is good for the pupil. When he has learnt to obey, it is well, both for him and for others, to learn if the path that he has chosen is one that is suited to him. First instructions, then, take in those who are to go on, and those who are to remain by the wayside, or who may turn into other paths. Meanwhile a lower average of instruction must necessarily be kept to, where so many are included.

It is also certain that the better the earlier *training*, the more certain and easy will be the later *culture*. There must be good grammar schools, there must be good preparatory education for those who, looking to the less fixed culture to be gained through the university, will need at first some definite discipline, even though it may be rigid or narrow, that they may be steadied for the greater liberty that shall open before them, when, as in the teachings of universities, they are shown the contradictions of systems of knowledge, and, for the advantage of their present and their future, are made acquainted with the diversity of the past.

The schools, therefore, which exist for the advantage of the beginner, and which are based upon an exclusive adherence to a single teaching, are necessary. Such considerations as our present course will open to us could not be approached, and certainly could not be understood, without a fair practical acquaintance with the ordinary grammar of the art of painting. What we wish to consider together is this: what freedom there may be in the application of the tools which we have learnt to use. Instead of an alphabet of letters, instead of a knowledge of the meaning of words taken separately, we wish to see how we can assemble these different parts that constitute our speech, and use them for that form of communication which is best suited to individual capacities. In the study of literature, in the study of the use of written words, we should be shown how men whose success had been more or less established by time, managed the mechanism of language.

Examples of well-used language would be laid before us, and we should be called upon to take lessons from them, and to admire the felicity of a success whose means we could now begin to understand. From all this acquaintance with the past we should gather a knowledge of the limitations attending any particular development, and of the extent and powers of such uses of the ordinary means that are common to all of us. Each individual mind would find some particular food best suited to its essential constitution; nor should we fear that an intimate knowledge of what had before been done by man would hamper us; except in the sense that all knowledge is a weight to carry, as is all baggage, as is all food, as are all means of protection and all engines of survey and of industry. Not only do we obtain, then, a useful material, but our minds are enlarged by having to fit into spaces larger than those we knew before; and the fact that these works of men which we study or admire contain, in some mysterious way, the informing principle which shaped them, brings us into a warm and living contact with the being of their makers. We gain some of their life; we are carried forward by their desires.

Nor does it matter that these things done are the work of men of whom we speak as no longer living. They are always the work of the majority of men; for the dead outnumber the living. And we are as close to human nature when with them, as we are to the human nature that moves for this brief moment around us. Some of these men live in books. In places like this Museum, we know them in painting or in sculpture, — in the forms of art more especially called *art*, because, perhaps, in painting and in sculpture, we see more distinctly with the results the many means employed by that desire of man which causes him to make what we call the beautiful. In our art of painting, above all others, that desire of the beautiful is expressed and appeased by representation of what is exterior — what is perceived by the sense of sight. Through these representations, more or less complete, more or less the result of acquired ideas, or, on the other

hand, of personal impressions, the artist has expressed what is in reality himself. If we were
gifted with the imaginary perception that we
attribute to supernatural beings, we could see
written out at length, in these works of art, not
only the character of their authors, but their
momentary feelings, often contradictory to the
apparent intention; and even their physical fail-
ings — the make and habit of their bodies.

Our form of art appears the most impersonal
of all to the perceptions of those who look upon
its results; and yet they and we usually satisfy
our feelings by applying to the work and its
methods adjectives implying moral or intellectual merits or demerits. Hence we speak of the
nobility of a man's style; hence we speak of the
sincerity of a work of art.

In reality, as I was saying, the art of painting
is perhaps less discreet than any other. It gives
most indubitable testimony of the moral state
of the painter at the very moment that he
used his brush. He has done what he wished
to do. If he has wished in a weak way, it is

possible to know it through various forms of in-
decision. All the more, that which he has not
really desired is absent from his work, — whatever he may say, whatever he may claim, whatever he may think, and whatever other people
may say about him. Any distraction, any manner of forgetfulness, a less warm impression, a
less deep and reaching application of sight, any
lessening of industry, any lessening of his love
for that which he is studying, the fatigue of
painting and the passion of painting, — all these
shades of his nature, even to the intermittent
action of his sensitiveness — all that is spread
out manifestly, whether we recognize it or not,
in the works of a painter, as sharply if he had
taken us into his confidence.[1]

For the thought that makes the work of art,
the thought which in its highest expression we
call genius, is not reflection or reflective thought.
The thought which analyzes has the same deficiencies as our eye. It can only fix one point
at a time. It is necessary for it to examine each

[1] Paraphrased from Fromentin.

element of consideration, and unite it to others,
to make a whole. But the logic of *free life*,
which is the logic of art, is like that logic of
our using the eye, in which we make most wonderful combinations of momentary adaptation, by
co-ordinating innumerable memories, by rejecting
those that are useless or antagonistic; and all
without being aware of it, so that those especially who most use the eye, as for instance the
painter, or the hunter, are unaware of more than
one single, instantaneous action.

The exercise of reasoning alone, which is our
usual way of defining thought, is, as I have just
been saying in regard to the eye, a limitation;
a limitation distinctly perceptible when we understand with difficulty what others understand
at once. And it may be that in the higher uses
of certain processes of reasoning, where a very
high life has acted in the way that I should
like to call genius, the effort has been so simple
and so natural that the memory of the multitudinous memories implied has passed away.
Take, for instance, that charming story told by

Biot, the astronomer, in his account of his studies
with Laplace. The great man had confided to
him his manuscripts of the "Mécanique Céleste,"
and for a long time the young student had
puzzled over some passage which began, "It is
easy to see that, etc." To him it was not easy
to see. After long study he had the courage to
explain his inability to his great patron, who
looked over the ancient notes and memoranda,
and said, "Well, I don't understand it either,
but there was a moment, while I was at work,
when it seemed so simple as not to be worth
analyzing." Still more so in a work of art,
executed through the body and appealing to
the mind through the senses, the entire make-up
of its creator addresses the entire constitution of
the man for whom it is meant.

Thus in any museum we can see certain great
differences in things; which are so evident, so
much on the surface, as almost to be our first
impressions. They are the marks of the places
where the works of art were born. Climate;
intensity of heat and of light; the nature of the

earth; whether there was much or little water in proportion to land; plants, animals, surrounding beings, have helped to make these differences; as well as manners, laws, religious and national ideals. If you recall the mere general physical impression of a gallery of Flemish paintings and of a gallery of Italian masters, you will have carried off in yourself two distinct impressions, each one the sum of all the impressions received during their lives by the men of these two races. The fact that they used their eyes more or less is only a small factor in this enormous aggregation of influences received by them and transmitted to us. Outside of those qualities of our minds which place us in sympathy with what these things mean, which make us admire them, which make us feel that we like them, which lead us to forget these foreign accents, lies a large domain of relation more or less accessible, very often almost impossible for us to appreciate. There must always be some sides in the work of a Greek more natural to a Greek than they are to us; even when the thoughts and modes of life of his race have become, by study and acquired memories, an intimate part of our own existence. How much more must it be so when we look at the works of art of another great civilization such as that of China and Japan. We are cut off from the vast amount of associations that have informed the lives of their makers. It is as if we read Shakespeare for the first time, in a language little understood of us. On that side, then, it is evident — even through our not being able to understand thoroughly — that there is something intangible in this physical object, something infinitely mysterious.

And if we have lost so many things, which in some cases are lost forever, of what seemed to the makers of works of art in the past the very essence of their difference from other people, what other things do we not lose when, for example, in poetry, the exact quality of a single vowel, its shading in the scale of sound, has so much expression, so much importance to us? Think of all the combinations of these simple elements in the style of a great poet. Each syllable has a personality of its own, yet exists only through the word which contains it. Each word has an enormous value, and yet has none by itself, but only as inserted in the statement which itself is part of the sentence, for the sentence is a whole, in the manner of the organism of a living body.

Style might be called a living form which the live spirit wraps around itself. The art of writing contains, then, a certain science which as yet it has not been fully conscious of; but what notions for our own art are hinted at by this mere glance at the mechanism of another art still more unconscious than our own! In our art of painting the forms of the language are more universal; more easily, therefore, can we understand this statement of Fromentin the painter:

"Should you take away from the paintings of Rubens the spirit, the variety, the peculiar fitness of any touch of the brush, you would take away a statement that carries weight — some necessary accentuation. Perhaps you might be taking away the one element which spiritualizes all this heavy matter, and transfigures so many and so frequent uglinesses; and that would be because you would suppress all his real sensitiveness, and, retracing effects to their first cause, you would kill the very life of the picture — you would make over a picture that had no soul. I could almost say that with each vanishing touch would disappear a personal feature of the artist."

If, then, the very surface of the paint does, in the work of a great and skilful painter, literally embody his feeling, even more than the arrangement and cadence of words carry out a poet's feeling, he becomes impossible to imitate in his personality, unless through a similar sentiment — as every one who has copied knows. Of course the acquirements that he has memorized in common with others — the principles from which he works — these not being subject to fluctuation, to moral and spiritual tides — these can be common property.

Hence it is that the search in common for certain truths, for certain qualities, constitutes a real school, as distinct from a set of imitators. The Dutchmen tried together for the same things,

for what has been called a portraiture of nature; for accuracy and subtlety of painting
upon an accuracy and subtlety of drawing which
serves as a base. Yet Ruysdael is as different
from Cuyp as shadow is from sunshine; and his
grave and solemn mind gives to the simplest and
most commonplace of landscapes a look of sad importance, which is almost like a reproach of light-
mindedness, addressed to any other man's work
which happens to hang alongside. He is said to
be almost impossible to copy — and yet his touch
is not elegant nor facile; his very dryness would
seem so slow that its motions could be followed by
any patient hand.

Certainly Jean François Millet was no unerring
and absolute painter like the great Dutchmen;
yet his name is recalled to me by the severity of
the mind of Ruysdael. The varying completeness
of his pictorial work, its frequent arbitrary decision, its exposing of the most interior mechanism
of his methods, might lead us to think that he
could be imitated with some success; but no one
who has attempted to do so has been able to repeat

the trial. The man in Millet the painter is too distinctly behind the work. According to his own view also, perhaps an excessive and a Spartan one, this was as it should be. When a friend of mine, who painted as well as any man of his school in the Paris of that day, came to Millet, to lay all this accomplishment at his feet and ask for direction, "It is well," said Jean François, "and you can paint.—But what have you to say?" ("Qu' avez-vous à dire?") What Millet had to say was based on the simplest of foundations. Enemies often, and doubtful friends sometimes, made of him a preacher of social change, a person who used painting as a manner of preaching some newer doctrine. In reality Millet could meet again in mature life the good village priest who had first taught him, and in answer to questioning, assure him that he still read in his Christian Bible habitually, and in his Virgil sometimes. And perhaps he could remember the old priest's quoting, in an old-fashioned way, the sentences of the great French bishop, who was also the great French preacher. They run something like this. He is describing the time that saw the end of Roman liberty, and the establishment of universal empire, and he says, "Jesus Christ was born, and God gave to the Romans the empire of *this world*, as a gift of little price." In the thought behind these words you will see the acceptance of suffering and of effort in patience, as part of the ordering of the world. Should we read habitually our Christian Bible in that meaning, not unmindful of the Sermon on the Mount, not untouched by the sad sweetness of Virgil, we should be nearer to being able to work in the spirit represented by Millet.

It is hard to leave off speaking of men whose praise is a benediction to the speaker, and to pass, as we have engaged to do, into a consideration of works behind which the man is covered up or in hiding. Museums are also receptacles for a class of works, examples difficult to define by analysis, as they are difficult to define in their reality, unless we speak of them as not belonging personally to their makers. In the forms of art that deal with words such a classification becomes almost hopeless, and we can see the reason of

it more distinctly after we have considered the
question in our own art, wherein analysis and
separation of the intention and the method is
apparently easier. And still the question I wish
you now to consider is not an easy one to solve,
and when it is sought out in individual examples
it never can be absolutely disentangled from the
personal equation of the artist, so true is the
view that we have been considering, which makes
a work of art an expression of the man. This
difficulty has been beautifully expressed by the
painter whom I quoted before (and who is represented as a painter on the walls of our
Museum), Fromentin :

" Any work of art which has been deeply felt
by its maker is also naturally well-painted. And
any work of art in which the hand reveals itself
in felicity or in splendour is through that alone
a work belonging to the brain, or has its origin
in it."

To many people, art is a trade merely more
difficult than others. The artist to them is a
person who plays with certain tools, delighting

in the skill which he can display in using them. But that is to confuse art with the processes of art. It is true that the artist, more especially the sculptor and the painter, is a workman; and that view of himself is a healthy one for him, the more literally he holds it. It might save him, if he really believed in it, from frequenting the houses of the rich and fashionable, and losing therein his personal dignity. It would keep him from being accessible to the influences of the moment, of changing fashion, all the more felt in idle life, and destructive of higher taste and style.[1] Anything which will help his remaining humble will keep his work fresh as coming from himself alone. In reality, confusion may occur in his mind, and in ours too; because his workmanship and his efforts in it are inseparable from his inclination to it. The child, for instance, stutters before it speaks. Its intentions and desires, little by little, form its language. And art is a language — a language made on

[1] Cf. Viollet le Duc's explanation of the difficulty of the artist's preserving style to-day, unless through isolation.

purpose for the thought it tries to express. The statement of Fromentin is fully sufficient. It is not that the methods, the workmanship, can be detached from thought, but that the methods are so intimately connected with it, are such a necessary instrument of it, that they make one thing.

We can see what really happens when processes —methods—are separated from sentiment. How often have we heard, how often have we read : such and such a painting is in the first, the second, the third style of the artist. It is frequently possible to divide the periods of artistic production, and in its lower forms the life of the artist very often runs in this way: In his first period he learns his methods, re-creating them for his own special use. In the second — more or less a master of them — through them he expresses himself, his life, his creation of the world in his mind. In the third — through some decadence of internal life, some loss of that vital faculty which exists in all men, and which, in its highest sense, we call genius, but which is simply the power of organizing ideas, images, signs, without employing the slow processes of apparently consecutive thought: — by some beginning of death, then, he no longer expresses himself, but repeats the methods which he has invented; or which, in certain cases, he has partly assimilated from others. And these methods, having once been intimately connected with interior life, recall, through the ordinary action of memory, the impression of a vitality once connected with them; so that he is often unconscious of the fact that all that he gives is these methods belonging to his own past, which no longer express him as he is to-day. He is then dead, — emptied. The exterior vase remains; the contents have run out. Many a man has died on making the discovery.[1] The Baron Gros — after a brilliant career, which largely affected French art, and whose last and greater echoes died out in one of the greatest of painters, Delacroix — drowned himself. Lemoine, a fashionable and successful painter of the middle of the eighteenth century, suspecting a decay which no one else had yet

[1] Séailles.

recognized, ran himself through with his sword.
With the works produced at these moments of
an artist's life the galleries and collections of the
world are full. Sometimes they puzzle us; usually
we pass them by.

And the history of art shows us, again, numbers of artists who, grouped around some greater
men, imitate their processes, as in the full belief
that all that there is of art is process, or what
is sometimes called technique.

The greater man has made the dress he wears
as the birds make their plumage. The imitator
imitates the dress. Often, for a short time, fame,
success, fortune, attend the imitator; he is sometimes, for a time, more famous than the original
he imitates. At length, with time, we cannot
understand how this success was ever possible.
Have any of you seen — and I suppose you have
— the works of the painters who formed the end
of the school of David? What do you think
you would feel if you could be transported back
to that date, and saw the Salon of, let us say,
the year 1819? And yet the artists whose works

would seem so uninteresting to you were intelligent men, full of knowledge of the methods
they employed; and nobody around them gave
them an idea that a time would come when the
very existence of their names would be a bore.
And many of us who laugh at them are no
better men than they. They belonged to their
time; they applied current formulas, the methods
of work of that day; but these processes were
not the result of powerful conviction, the expression of their own sentiment, a co-ordination of
the memories of sight in a personal equation.
They were mostly the records of the memories
of the likings of certain processes. If processes
still look fresh and interesting in the masters,
it is because these processes are intimately connected with personal sentiment. It is not so
with the imitators. Once upon a time, the fashionable form which they employed was associated, in the minds of those about them, with
the memories of certain ideas, certain views, certain feelings. Whenever, at that time, these
forms and methods were used by them, these

associated memories were recalled; now, to-day, they can no longer make our memories act. We still, however, can feel a certain pleasure, a certain curiosity, in these forms by themselves, abstracted, if I may so say, from the more important parts of the work of art. I suppose that we recognize a certain logic, a certain fitness of the structure which holds together, perhaps somewhat as we like the balance of adjustment of the costumes of certain old periods. We can't wear them, and we wouldn't wear them; but they hold together in a certain way. This, of course, I suppose to be quite apart from the charm we receive from memories of the past — memories which already must be records of the memories of others.

There are examples of works of art, which again fill spaces in museums, where there is no pleasure in looking upon the process, where the process has been a poor one originally, and where we can hardly realize, so poor it is, that it is an imitation. In fact, we only realize that it is an imitation because of the apparent impossibility

that any strong feeling should not show, even in
a contradictory way, to such a weak use of material.   Of course I am now speaking of the testimony of the work itself.   In judging of the works
of painters, or of the schools, we help ourselves by
comparison and by a knowledge of what has been
done at the time.

Though it is extremely difficult to make out
their origin, the failures, the works of art that
have missed their point, might allow us to distinguish more clearly what there may be of laws in
art that should not be infringed.   Before them we
are no longer under the spell of the undefinable,
and that side of criticism which is the easiest, because it remains only a matter of judgment and a
cold-blooded investigation, can be used without disturbance, under the pressure of a certain indigna-
tion or disappointment.

It may happen that works which the slow
development of artistic judgment has gradually
condemned have been for a time just those which
would please the ordinary mind ; or have been
made to suit the commonplace critics, who wish

to have *all rules* carried out of which they *know*, and who are fond of settling for good and for all what shall be done.   By the ordinary mind I mean a certain manner of looking at things, on the part of people who consider a work of art as made to suit something that they wish noted, something that they care for at the time.   When that time is over, and they themselves, or their children, have changed their views, the interesting work of art meant expressly to suit them and their ideas is liable, having contained little else, to be passed over as stupid and meaningless.

Most of the work done to embody the feelings of the moment, according to the fashion of feeling at the moment, loses its meaning later.   If the moment be a grand one, with little fashion or momentary manner, the meaning remains proportionately grand.   Many of the so-called historical pictures which embody official enthusiasm, the marriages of kings and queens, the proclamations of certain edicts, the winning of certain battles, have little artistic interest for us to-day, as far as their main character is concerned ; and it

is only when some fact of archæology, some average portraiture, can be rescued from them, that
we think of them at all in the sequence of the
history of art.

And so it has been for an enormous mass of
works of art destined for the use of religion; more
properly, perhaps, for the use of the clergy, or
for personal satisfaction of certain types of the
religious mind, in which works Art has been so
completely the Handmaid of Religion, that to-day
— a day of other wishes and requests — looks
upon them as void of religious feeling. And so
they are, as far as art is concerned; because art
alone can carry from age to age the personal feeling of the artist, through which alone he can
express religious feeling. Of course at the time
many such things — I mean such points to be
observed by the artist, to suit his patron — were
matters of great consequence; that is to say, they
were matters of great consequence in the general
world, which is a world of momentary views
and necessities; not in the world of art. If the
artist felt these things himself, and saw in them

elements for the building and formation of his
work, then, however much we may have lost the
intention of the patron or of the public which
the artist tried to please, there still remains the
evidence of his likings; there still remain the
other less transient truths which appealed to him
as an artist. To-day, far removed as we are from
the external agitation that troubled the theologies
of the seventeenth century, we cannot be moved,
as many a clergyman then was, by the figure of
the crucified Christ, represented as hanging rigidly
from His uplifted arms, thereby, to a person who
looked upon art as merely a handmaid of religion,
appearing to have died for the few and not for
all; because the latter idea required outstretched
arms. You will see that this special verity, if
I may so call it out of respect for others, which
the theologian cared for, is not the sort of verity
which art can best embody. It needs explanation
and support outside of the statement concerning
it made by the artist.

As I spoke, a moment ago, of the so-called historical pictures of official importance, I remem-

bered a name connected with official honours, with
official academic honours, with official military
honours, with the voluntary admiration of the
men of his time. I can see myself long ago, a
young fellow, sensitive about my admiration, and
yet with all due respect for authority, spending
some of the first hours of my Parisian life in a
Parisian studio frequented by well-known men,
and one influenced by the great French power
known as l'École des Beaux-Arts. Visitors and
artists were discussing the impertinence of a
critic who had dared to attack the great Horace
Vernet, formerly President of the French Academy,
consequently a living part of the great French
government school, and a man liked by all, even
by those to whom he was unjust, and whose
names, being to-day more famous than his own,
you all know by heart. The question of personal
satisfaction for such insults to such a man in such
a school, ran through the day. The case of this
painter, so much liked, so much admired at that
time and long before, is a type of one of the very
many divisions into which we can separate those

forms of works of art which we are now considering, — those forms whose charm is gone, presum-
ably forever, and over which, if we have patience,
we can talk in cold blood.

To younger men this fame of the great military
painter is only a hearsay. It has not been continued with them; yet its testimony is written out in
the gigantic paintings which cover acres of surface
in the French galleries and museums. It is not
possible to characterize them in a few words.
They escape any very exact definition, within a
short compass. Their methods — their technique
— are simply the current processes of the day,
neither better nor worse; what is more or less
taught in the schools, with certain mildly ambi-
tious attempts made long after the great attempts
of the century had been made by others — by men
not of the school, in feeling at least.

As to the feeling, the poetry of these works of
art, some of you may have seen it in innumerable
pictures by all sorts of people. There is one well-
known painting of Vernet, perfectly expressing
the type, — the dead body of a lancer, lying so

flat that we are supposed to be on his level; and above him his horse, of the approved cavalry type, which waves one leg over him, and puts down its head towards him in affection and personal regret. Somewhere else, as a less important member of a theatrical troupe, a little dog barks. This, and similar pictures by him or by others, have naturally inundated the world. The great battle pictures I should prefer to have you go and see yourself, rather than attempt to think them over again. But I think that you would enjoy with me the small work, — the illustrations made for books by this important man, at night, at moments of leisure, during the progress of large works, — which show what he really was, how he had kept from boyhood all such good-natured likings as a boy might have — a delight in animals, a delight in soldiers; which likings, being those of a boy, were best expressed and rendered in his little drawings and sketches and lithographs, which are as full as his big and illustrious paintings are empty.

His error, then, had been to consider that he

was obliged to do great things; and we might
speak of him as a man who had mistaken his
scale. Of course this is only an intellectual mistake, perhaps a little of a moral one; looked at
from another point of view, the companion of
kings and emperors, and great people of all kinds,
the head of one of the greatest schools in the
world, a man known to everybody, from the greatest painters to the last school-boy or the sweep
who gazed at pictures in shop-windows, — that
man might be called a great success. And it
seems, or ought to seem, very sad that probably
few of you young people have heard of him.

Nor has the attempt to make a successful
work of art, by carrying out rules taken from
the outside — taken from academies or professors
of the beautiful, given to the work of art any
longer life. No genius for painting has ever
been given by a knowledge of perspective or a
theory of colour. The usual belief, the proverbial
one, is the belief that we all come to, that rules
exist for art, not art for rules.

To study any living thing we take it to pieces,

and usually discover its machinery more distinctly in death. A readjustment and juxtaposition of the elements that constituted life does not give life again and make a living unity. The work made by the reflective and analytic capacity is entirely comprehended by that same capacity, but before the work of genius, the living work, as before life itself, we are not able to express adequately our sensations, nor can our reason feel sure of a complete analysis. We feel that the charm that took hold of our soul has not been sufficiently conveyed through our words. And yet that charm has made us believe that we understood it. We have never been conscious of any effort. That effort, which some minds might take for admiration, is what we feel in presence of works of exterior importance in regard to technique, or practice unallied to feeling. But the effort ends in a feeling of offence, whose cause is that sort of coldness which irritates us in the dilettante. His manner is calculated for its effects upon us ; what we see in him and he wishes us to see, is not himself as he is, but the clever man he wishes to appear. He is afraid to give himself away, forgetting, as I said before, that he cannot help it. If he arranges himself, if he thinks of himself, though we do not discern him clearly in reality, we see that he is trying to impose upon us.

If he is skilful in his technique and methods, we observe, in a variety of purely intellectual pleasure, what he was after, and how he has done it. It is as if we followed the reasonings and excuses that he has made out for himself, and which we approve of or otherwise as we do of the carrying out of a school exercise.

But all the time we are fully aware of the fact that there may be more art — that there is more art — in the play of a child than in the careful structure of many a learned verse-maker.

Let there be no misunderstanding: Art is not a lawless game: even want of power in the artist puts up unwillingly with incorrection, unless he be deceived by vanity. In his work the real man forgets himself and any small pride — clearly or obscurely feeling that to try to find originality is a sure way of losing one's path.

In all of the greatest artists there is a humble workman who knows his trade and likes it. Art is a language and has a grammar that varies only as languages vary — and for its practice there must be an acquired facility, a certain combination of observed laws. Upon many of its departments the cooler reason can pronounce. There are questions even in such complex matters as composition, in such delicate matters as unity and sequence of thought, where reasoning finds its place. But tendency and enthusiasm precede work. "Genius," says the French phrase, "is a protracted patience." (Le génie est une longue patience.) It can only keep up its life by continuous effort, often by work so exclusive as to make all other ideas of life disappear. But we must remember that we are so enslaved by the idea of time which we measure in small instalments, according to other necessities, that we do not perceive that these efforts are really one single act — the act of life. The artist has this consciousness more exactly than we have, however obscurely, and feels not so distinctly the succession of his efforts as their general tendency.

And so for the work that he carries out, he rarely sympathizes with the surprise — still less with the admiration of the outside world, which speaks of the length of time that such a work of art has cost. Be it a short moment or a term of years, it has cost the same thing, i.e. the whole man.[1] When he steps into the outside world he can see the matter gauged by other measurements. As a good citizen, as a family man, as working for a patron, he can divide what he has done into some succession of efforts. . . . In the progress of his life at first there is the instinct, the inherited disposition; then the accumulated memories of images, which give him a language for his sentiment. The tend-

[1] Cf. Mr. Whistler's well known answer in court. "Question: 'The labour of two days, then, is that for which you ask two hundred guineas?' Answer (Mr. Whistler): 'No. I ask it for the knowledge of a life-time.'" Also the answer of Kiosai, the Japanese artist. When exception was taken to the price he had put upon his painting of a crow, he replied: "This is not a price for a painting of a crow, but a price for my hard study for several tens of years."

ency to translate these by the hand decides the destiny of the painter. But his instinct is not like that of lower forms of life, apparently fixed in a structure definitely adjusted. For each new work he has to readjust himself. Through long work he tends more and more to fix the tendencies of heredity or individual chance. He prepares the instrument which shall answer, by an impressive sign, the motion of his mind. Thus will the musician study harmony, composition, the masters of the past, so as not to have to think separately of them; so as to create a world of memories which dispense him from reflective action, and become as a habit, that he may be fully free when the time comes for action.

This free world that he creates escapes the chances of the exterior world in which he lives. And it is that world of his into which we enter, really taking part in its making over again. For the pleasure given by art is not a passive one. We give it to ourselves. It has been well said that what we call taste is a

real art. The work of art may remain silent
to many; even to those who understand it
more or less. It is an appeal to another mind,
and it cannot draw out more than that mind
contains. But to enjoy is as it were to
create; to understand is a form of equality, and
the full use of taste may be a work of genius.

We each see in the work of the artist a work
more or less different according to our natures.
Nor can we enjoy equally all works of art.
We cannot at will take up all the postures of
the mind of another. But we are not under
an illusion when we feel pride in the enjoyment of beauty; and they are excusable who
feel as if they had made the work which they
admire. They become, for an instant, the man
who made it and who is at his best very
often; and they feel that they are better than
themselves. The artist whom we admire cannot
be indifferent to us; witness the way in which
we take his part, often with more zeal than
he would have had himself; because for the
moment it is in us and owing to us that his

work lives. During these moments we, the spectators, live a serene and complete existence.

And so, by melting one's self into the methods and the reasons for the methods of masters, one would feel less inclined to have one's own way; which is very different from going in one's own way. And we students, we who study together, may see that originality does not consist in looking like no one else, but merely in causing to pass into our own work some personal view of the world and of life.

If you have understood me, you will see that all these are *men* whom you learn to know;—and there is little else that counts. Yet as they are part of nature, which may be defined for you to be what lies outside of yourself, and not your own consciousness — so what they have done is a part of nature. And in fact, most of that nature seen by their eyes would not have been seen by you had it not been for them. Each of the greater ones, each of the greater schools, has chosen some part of the world of sight to insist upon and delight in. The even blue sky not fully lit, in which float masses of grey and golden cloud, recalls to us painters the name of Veronese.

"To bathe all, even light itself, in a bath of shadow, from which it might emerge more wet and more glimmering; to make these waves of obscurity sweep around the lit surfaces; to vary, to deepen and to thicken the flood, and yet to make obscurity visible and shadow easy to see through" — such was the method of Rembrandt, in which he worked with a perfection so complete that even nature's use of similar mystery bears his name.

LECTURE II

PERSONALITY AND CHOICE

SYNOPSIS OF LECTURE II.

Examples of original artistic life beginning from study of works of art. — The memories and practice of the studio necessarily carried out of doors. — Danger of confusion of practices with principles. — Methods are but tools. — There is no absolute way of painting. — The artist is judged by the appreciation of the way he looks upon the world. — There is no absolute nature : there can be no absolute view of nature. — Practically there is no such thing as Realism. — How differently painters might look at the same subject. — For each variation some special translation by the hand : for each variation by the hand some modification in the use of materials.

LECTURE II.

PERSONALITY AND CHOICE.

In my first lecture I said that the various considerations announced in our beginning, should be repeated in various ways, from different points of view, as they will lead us gradually to all the points of study which you can require, and might even help us to the furthest and finest details of processes or of what is sometimes called technique.

You will remember that we divided works of art into two large classes, making the division by their essential constitutions.

In the one we placed works in which the artist had used the personal combination of all possible factors; showing us how he expressed his view of the world, how he had seen, with what body and senses, what hereditary manners, what memories of acquired liking, what development of memory through study, and what personal colouring.

In the other division we had placed those who had used *part* of these means, and noticed that this division would contain things by imitators of such works as those just classed, who only used a *part* of these means of memory.

We saw how in the former works the artist had expressed *himself*. We noticed that the search in common for certain truths, for certain qualities, constituted a real school, as distinct from a set of imitators.

As an example of great value I cited the Dutch school: and in that school, bound together by very strict interpretation of nature — by what has been called a portraiture of nature, — I reminded you how different Cuyp was from Ruysdael, and how distinct and individual was Ruysdael's character within the methods of the school.

I also cited Millet in connection with Ruysdael, and pointed out the former as a type of a most distinct expression of personality seen through and behind methods. We then passed from ex-

amples of the full life of the artist to examples
of deficient representation, such as are shown in
the works of imitators, such as are shown in the
works of those who work for the public, and to
meet the desires of others, which are not fully
their own.

I cited certain types of official painting, of historical pictures and so-called religious pictures;
and among historical painters, so-called, I referred
to the former fame of Horace Vernet, and to the
particular error represented by him, that of mis-
application of scale, he having been a charming
designer in small, an excellent book illustrator
and caricaturist, while his big and once famous
paintings have come to be considered empty failures.[1] The cause of the error of works of art

[1] I took the famous Horace only as a type which happened to be
handy — not as a prominent or necessary example.

You will remember how I referred to the theatrical quality of some
of his work. This theatrical element enters somewhat into many
works of art, and must always have been an element. We see it, for
example, in the works of Hokusai, the Japanese, where it distorts the
expression of his love of nature.

But it may be worth noting in the direction of our reflections of
last week, that the fashion of the theatre changes, and that to-day the
opera expression of fifty years ago, reflected in pictures, looks rather

based upon academic formulas was then considered, the cause being the impossibility of building together the elements of a work of art which had been obtained through cold-blooded dissection of former living masterpieces.

Certain insufficiencies of mere technique were considered in various ways, to be summed up in the usual belief that rules and methods exist for art — not art for rules.

An analysis was given of the growth of the painter, from his earliest tendencies to the studies which allow him to be himself. In this work created by him as a mere mode of life, we are able to live in the world that he has made, and to enjoy it, and in a certain way to make it over ourselves; because enjoyment is another form of creation, and taste is a form, perhaps, of genius. In this existence in common with the painter there is a form of study which could be completed by

absurd to us, who are accustomed to more complex and studied staging. So later the Wagnerian influence will seem as absurd, and theatrical solemnities of to-day reflected in painting will appear as they are in reality, stage arrangements made to suit a very average taste — for which we are all a little responsible.

effort, so as to bid good-bye to such a narrow view
as having one's own way; and to obtain the real
originality of walking in one's own *path;* and to
express what art is meant for: the representation
of the artist's view of the world. And the works
of the past, having been made by man, who is a
part of nature, and nature being what is outside
of us, these works of art are parts of nature. And
indeed, each great artist and each great school has
chosen some part of nature which is subject to
sight, as a matter of study and delight; so that
without them it might be said that we should not
have learned to see nature in those details: as,
for instance, the light in which Veronese painted,
which we artists recognize in the sky of certain
days; and the methods of the chiaroscuro of Rembrandt, so completely stated by him in his paintings, that his name is attached to this expression
of nature herself.

In such admiration of certain men, in some
realization of how they have seen certain sides of
nature, we see nature better — we see it limited,
if I may so say, prepared for us, so that we

can take hold of it — grasp it — enjoy it without confusion.

At the same time, we can rejoice in their rendering, and in an artistic development continue it; if we do so sincerely, not as imitators but as enjoyers, we can find for ourselves some corner of these great pasturelands which will or may become our own.

In any such study, any such delight, it is possible to extend one's self in a personal development which might almost make us — those of us who are not the makers, disbelieve in the fact of such a new and true life having been begun from mere works of art.

Thus the group of French artists whose general tendencies are most splendidly represented by Rousseau, the landscape painter, began to see nature, the ordinary French nature around them, with young and fresh eyes, with newly discovered interests, almost as if they had found a new world at their very doors, without forgetting, for a long time, the impression of the great Dutchmen. The conventionalities of Holland helped them to discover France. They began with admiration of the portrait feeling of the Dutch, with the Dutch acceptance of things as they were, with what seemed to them a departure from the arbitrary classicality of their own French school. They admired and they imitated the solidity of make of these northern paintings, as well as the placidity of their subjects, the apparent absorption of the artist in his result, and they began by imitating the surfaces of these representations of nature. With a man like Rousseau, continually in love with each thing that he saw, unwilling to eliminate or simplify, because he could not put aside one love for another, the result became as complex, as multitudinous, as the results of the Dutchmen's likings were simple and self-contained.

But throughout, wherever, as is necessary in painting, which is eminently a conventional art, there were passages in nature that reminded him of his old loves in Holland — I mean the Holland of pictures; wherever he had to supply, as we all have, the insufficiency of observation by the habit of mechanism, there Rousseau's filiation from the

Dutch is evident and often beautiful. He holds the past by the hand, however far he may stretch towards newer gains, newer ambitions, unknown, or apparently unknown, to his more peaceful pictorial ancestors, the Dutch painters that he loved.

Corot, a greater lover of *Italy*, a less naïve lover of nature, less willing to accept all the blemishes of his beloved, and preferring to see her reflected in himself, passed away from these early tendencies, but never from their principle. Not the things themselves, but the spirit of the things became the object of his representation, and in that way, as Fromentin says, "No one can be so little of a Hollander."

But the origin of that great French school, — I use the word *school* as stating certain beliefs in common, and not objects in common — is Dutch; and Flers, Cabat, Dupré, Rousseau and Corot all began together a form of opposition in which their enemies felt the distrusted influence of a foreign school which had ended in a Rembrandt. They feared, not the opening of nature again — the École des Beaux-Arts did not look so

far as out-of-doors, but the possible triumph of a
school of colour and of light.

You will notice that this school of nature began
in the Museum, and that old Dutch pictures explained to young men that there was such a thing
as a French nature round about them. The impression made by the representation of that
nature concealed to the admirers of these men
the manner of the first steps taken towards this
discovery.

Such a freedom of sight, such personal life,
may therefore come from the admiration of
others. But often, when we look at certain
works of art, — and I mean the successful ones
— the complete ones, — we may decide that, so
far as we are concerned, what we see is complete;
that is to say that the thing is over, and that we
need to take for ourselves some other direction, to
explore some other less discovered country.

Occasionally this feeling takes an ugly form in
ugly people who say, "I don't like this; as for
me, I like that." But I am only talking of the
essence of a meaning, not of our saying and

thinking in an ugly way, which is only a way, and not the constitution of our thinking.

We may have such likings in studying nature (that is to say, as I have defined nature — all outside of us) through other artists, greater and more complete than ourselves; and yet it often happens that we need more than one man's view or one school's view, to be moved ourselves to action. We need some other admiration to fructify that first one, as if another element had to be added; as if the plant had flowered, but needed some favourable wind to carry to it from others what would make it fertile.

I am leaving out of consideration entirely that point of which so many young people are very proud, — the actual going out of one's own free will, seeing the things of nature and out-of-doors for one's self, and taking only from what one sees alone, unaided by any one's influence, — uninfluenced by any memories that one has ever known. This side we shall consider later; it will furnish us, I think, with surprises greater than any the strangest painter can ever give us.

But meanwhile, I may give you a premonition
of what we shall find. We can consider all
that we record in our brains as memories composed of many other memories. We can, therefore, see nothing without the use of the memory
of sight — or we should not know what it is.
Nor, as you know, could we judge of the relations of the things we see, without memories of
practice in observing relations.

Even for such a simple thing as knowing
that one thing is further than another we have
had to make many trials of the eye, and get
away from the early condition of the child who
puts out his hand to touch the moon.

And so for the use of our hand in painting,
and so for the use of our colours. When you
try to paint a colour or a tone that you see out-
of-doors you have to draw upon some practice
of mixing some colours together. Say it is a
blue sky — *some* use of *blue* has been made by
you ; and you have gone instinctively to the
colour-box to find the place you have in your
memory, the kind of colour you have in your

memory, the kind of mixture you have in your memory. Not once in millions of times do you see a thing painted as if the painter tried that combination of paints for the first time. Usually he has a recipe; he must have one, even if he has to abandon it for the moment.

Nothing is more ironical, therefore, to any one who has a set palette of certain pigments, than to suppose that he can be absolutely free-minded in the way he reproduces things. It is as if we said: We shall be free in the use of words, and if necessary, put in words of other languages — any which seem nearer, Japanese, Chinese, French; and as these cannot meet all cases, we shall invent them as we go along.

Of course we do arrange words, — combine them, combine their intonations, their sounds, their suggestions, and the memories they suggest, as well as their distinct and limited meanings. And we scramble through with these difficulties.

As to the painter, he does the same, feeling that his intention is the main thing, and trusting, without being conscious of that reliance, to the manner in which we the lookers-on help to make the illusion. For we make the illusion ourselves : — The painting has nothing for us but what we can co-ordinate of our memories. An Ashantee Negro or an average picture dealer cannot see a painting with the eye of a Rembrandt or a Rousseau, and make as great an illusion for himself.

When I look at the brush mark of a Japanese painter, — which is but a sweep of India ink, it may have for me modelling, colour, air, texture, the sense of weather, of wet, heat, or windy cold — a feeling of reticence or of fulness of detail. Between his few lines I will feel the water of the rushing waterfall or the wet surfaces of the rice fields.

The black etched line of Rembrandt will give me a far spreading horizon not in the direction of his line, but running to it. A few scratches of his will make the earth sink or rise, remain solid, or be covered with water : — no longer in fact be ink and paper, but light and air and shadow and varying form.

But of this further, when the time comes to consider how we see, which I hope to make you think of later. Meanwhile we may be sure that every-one carries out-of-doors some memories of the studio, and an enormous mass of acquired habits, partly not his own. Such studies and inquiries as we can follow will reassure us that there is a general direction always followed, even by artists who are not known to each other, who in their path might be said not even to be within calling distance. And we can clear our minds, and call things by their right names, and not confuse main principles with the various practices or methods necessary to *carry out* the principles in each varying case.

No; we artists must — whether we will it or not, whether we recognize it or not — be led by our individual being. We give our attention, then our likings, to some one, now caring for this one, now delighting in that one, and out of the practice of each one often getting without knowing it the essential principles held in each case and in common by each artist we have loved and admired in turn.

And sometimes, if instead of looking at the artist himself, i.e. his works, we listen too easily to talk about his work by others than himself (for he may be dead), we may be told that certain practices are principles — that certain habits are essential reasons.

In addressing you confidentially, I feel the occasional necessity of coming to anecdote and memories, so as to reinforce by actual single fact what I am saying, lest it should appear abstract and inapplicable.

I had rather not speak to you of myself and of other painters I know and have known. But the main value of what I have to say to you students and younger people is that I am older and have gone through many of your experiments of practice, your admirations or dislikes, and your trials of mind. They are new for each of us singly, as they come along, fresh as they were when the first man looked about him.

After all, remember that what I tell you is the result of life, whether in thought or in action; and that I am only able to give principles and foundations for thinking, through having visited certain regions of thought, through surprises that have fallen upon me, and that what confidence I have to-day in talking to you is based on no *a priori* certainty that I had it all before beginning.

And so certain little experiences of myself and others have been, in a sort of foreshortened manner, lessons to me and helps to thought. What has made me break off to say this to you just now is the coming back to my mind of an interview with a younger man. Some while ago a former assistant of mine in my work in glass called upon me, and in friendly talk — perhaps as a sort of confession — intimated to me that he had often been told that I was wrong in my principles, and that he had thought so himself; and that yet, when he had to judge of the results, he had found his advisers unable to attain them themselves, and that somehow or other my results were right.

I reminded him that I had never talked of principles to him at all, — that our relations

were mere matters of practice, he doing what I
told him to do, in so far as he could understand
what I asked for. And I repeated to him the
following story. Some years ago, while painting
Trinity Church in Boston, I employed for part
of the work a firm of New York decorators. It
so happened that, displeased with much that they
did, I left large spaces bare, with no indication
of my intention, which places I proposed deco-
rating through men whom I was training for
the purpose. One day the foreman of the firm,
himself a decorator, well known, I suppose, by
this time, came to me in anger and dismay,
and told me bluntly that I was working against
every principle of painting. As workmen are
always worth listening to when they speak sincerely of their trade — and I thought the man
a workman — I expected to get some important
information. But my man merely stated that
the painting of any room or interior should be
begun from the top, and go right down to the
bottom without interruption. Hoping for some
new point in optics, I questioned further and

asked why. Then he told me, with contempt
as well as anger, that otherwise some of the
lower work might get spotted by a workman,
and would need repairing and perhaps cost
money. This story gives the clue to a great
many methods which are used because they are
convenient and not because they are the best.
And thus I have sometimes relieved the minds
of conscientious students troubled by assertions
of principles, by drawing their attention to the
fact that there are trade methods which are con-
verted into principles by people whose interest
it is to confuse them, or whose minds have been
attuned to them at an early stage of development.

Even if this were a proper place, I should
not feel inclined to allow you to believe that
there was only one proper manner of carrying
out a work of art: that getting canvas of a
certain thickness and of a certain absorbent or
non-absorbent quality, and painting thereon with
a certain kind of brush, either a square one or
one of a different shape, and using with that

brush certain pigments bought at certain places in the city, from which certain colours are excluded, or among which they are included, and dropping that paint on in a certain way, controlled by the shape of the brush, and the manner in which the manufacturer made the canvas, is the proper method of painting.

Whatever I might myself believe, such a teaching as I have described would be absurd in a museum. Can you imagine the smile that would disturb the faces of the Egyptian mummies in the rooms below us, who may have known the sculptors that made the Walking Sheik El Beled, or the sweet face of the lady Nefert, or the terrible Chafra who sits at Boulak? The methods of to-day were unknown when these men lived, and yet who of to-day can hope to go any further? And what would Rembrandt think, and Veronese, and Rubens, and Velasquez? Surely these men painted as well as you can ever hope to paint, and each one in a different method, and each one admiring the others, wondering at the other's scope and the other's art.

Understand that what you have to learn here, where all things are gathered at the risk of every possible contradiction, is the size of the world and its being greater than any one personal experience.

The science of to-day, while it establishes more certainly many things which the artist who works in matters of sight has stated from personal certainty, makes us understand how wide are the variations within which these certainties are apprehended by the artist, and explains to us more and more the importance of his personal equation, shows us what we painters have always felt, — through what imperfect means and against what enormous odds the soul of the artist has tried to express itself. As we consider the history of the long struggle of the artist at expressing his likings of the outside world, from him who first scratched the outlines of the reindeer and the mastodon upon fragments of bone, — to Rembrandt or Velasquez who can deceive our eyes by films of superimposed colour, we see how accurately men have always felt, and how inaccurately they have seen. At the same time, with every inaccuracy has been blended some distinct proof of strong perception, which has been willing to *accept* certain *deficiencies*, that the main purpose of observation might be carried out triumphantly. Each man has succeeded in turn, through fitting his means to his capacity, that is to say, to the sum of memories accumulated in him by his ancestors and himself, and by using his very deficiencies to introduce us, as if by human sympathy, to the truths of impression that he valued most.

If any one should ever wish to give you a fixed equation that shall cover every problem of painting, without taking any account of *your* carrying it out, if any one gives you a general nostrum to be applied at once by yourself, remember what a hesitating artist once said to another kindly one, willing to impart to him, for his good, the absolute secret of Titian.

"It is all very evident," said the more prudent painter; "no doubt you have the complete formula; and you, in your strength, can apply it and paint works of art quite equal to the formula. But for me, I am a weakling, and I should stagger under such a heavy weight of certainties. I had rather carry a burden more suited to my back."

In such a place, then, as a museum, we may well look with awe at the long succession of efforts made by our ancestors in art, those whom we know and those whom we do not know, but from whom we inherit in common. It is to study some of these efforts, among which there may be some that will avail you, that we have come together. We are not anxious, at present, to place any exact date or sequence upon them, except as the one may strictly derive from the other. For our purposes, we may often be anxious, on the contrary, to forget their date and the place where they were made; because what is most interesting to us in the line of our proposed inquiry is that these artists of all kinds and degrees were men like ourselves, and had to work with means not dissimilar to ours.

Men, then, are all important; the ways in

which we paint or shall paint are the tools they have used or will use. It is well that you should admire how well these tools are adapted to their use; and if, moreover, they fit your hand, you do well to use them.

Though we do well to tend towards an absolute way of painting, there is no such thing if by painting we mean the representation of what can be noticed or seen. But there are wise ways and less wise ways — more generous ones — less narrow ones — more universal ones; some more personal, others more general. But each of these is based again on what the man intended. Of him we can judge as we judge men; and strange to say, it will always be more or less by a moral idea, by an appreciation of the way he looked upon the world.

And in the artist, have you ever noticed how simple it is to disentangle the man? When once the artist has summed up in himself the memories of his apprenticeship, the acquired memories of others, and his own, — derived from them perhaps, but at any rate added to them, — you can try with him the following experiment. Take him to ten different places; set him before ten different subjects; ask him to copy what he sees before him. I say to copy, so as to make our task of finding him out more easy. All of these so-called copies, which are really representations, will be stamped in some peculiar way, more or less interesting, according to the value of our artist. And you will recognize at once that they are really ten *copies of his manner of looking at* the thing that he copies.

Suppose again, that you could persuade ten different artists — I am speaking of artists, that is to say, of people who have already the use of the tools of their trade — ask — persuade these ten men to copy, as I have called it, the same subject in nature, the same landscape; and you will have ten different landscapes, in that you would be able to pick out each one for the way it was done. In short, any person who knew anything about it would recognize, as it were, ten different landscapes.[1]

[1] R. Töpfer.

Now we have, as it were, brought the question to a case so simple, to a trial so absolute, that anybody can understand it. And this trial, or a similar trial, is made over and over again, whenever two or three artists of any character have gone out sketching together. I remember myself, years ago, sketching with two well-known men, artists who were great friends, great cronies, asking each other all the time, how to do this and how to do that; but absolutely different in the texture of their minds and in the result that they wished to obtain, so far as the pictures and drawings by which they were well known to the public are concerned.

What we made, or rather, I should say, what we wished to note, was merely a memorandum of a passing effect upon the hills that lay before us. We had no idea of expressing ourselves, or of studying in any way the subject for any future use. We merely had the intention to note this affair rapidly, and we had all used the same words to express to each other what we liked in it. There were big clouds rolling over hills, sky clearing above, dots of trees and water and meadow-land below, and the ground fell away suddenly before us. Well, our three sketches were, in the first place, different in shape; either from our physical differences, or from a habit of drawing certain shapes of a picture, which itself usually indicates — as you know, or ought to know — whether we are looking far or near. Two were oblong, but of different proportions; one was more nearly a square ; the distance taken in to the right and left was smaller in the *latter* case, and on the contrary, the height up and down — that is to say the portion of land beneath and the portion of sky above — was greater. In each picture the distance bore a different relation to the fore-ground. In each picture the clouds were treated with different precision and different attention. In one picture the open sky above was the main intention of the picture. In two pictures the upper sky was of no consequence — it was the clouds and the mountains that were insisted upon. The drawing was the same, that is to say, the general make of things ; but each man had involuntarily looked upon what was most interesting to him in the whole sight; and though the whole sight was what he meant to represent, he had unconsciously preferred a beauty or an interest of things different from what his neighbor liked.

The colour of each painting was different — the vivacity of colour and tone, the distinctness of each part in relation to the whole; and each picture would have been recognized anywhere as a specimen of work by each one of us, characteristic of our names. And we spent on the whole affair perhaps twenty minutes.

I wish you to understand, again, that we each thought and felt as if we had been photographing the matter before us. We had not the first desire of expressing *ourselves*, and I think would have been very much worried had we not felt that each one was true to nature. And we were each one true to nature.

Of course there is no absolute nature; as with each slight shifting of the eye, involuntarily we focus more or less distinctly some part to the prejudice of others. And not only would this result

have been the same if we had gone on painting,
but had we made a drawing — had we made a
careful representation, or a rapid note of what we
saw by lines (that is to say, by an abstraction of
the edges of the surfaces that we saw), any one
could have told the names of the men who had
done it.

All this sort of thing is perfectly well known,
but on that very account you will have passed
over the importance of its meaning. You will
see again what I have been telling you, last week
and to-day, that the *man* is the main question,
and that there can be no absolute view of nature.
I do not know how often you may be talked to
about theories of art, and how much you care
for the same at the present moment; but at
some moment or other you will have brought
before you that most important conflict of realism
and its opposite. I don't say idealism, because I
don't so distinctly know what is meant by it;
while realism has been in the market now for
quite a time, and has served as a beautiful play-
ground for various intellects. What I want you

to notice is that though in abstraction there must be such a thing — I should be the last to gainsay it — yet, in these realities with which we are concerned, realism is a very evasive distinction. If the experiments that I spoke of — if experiences such as I have just related about myself and others bring out the result that you have seen, there is for you practically no such thing as realism.

You need not, therefore, be afraid of the word; you need not be afraid of indulging the illusion that you are rendering the real reality of the things that you look at — that you are copying, that you are transcribing. If you ever know how to paint somewhat well, and pass beyond the position of the student who has not yet learned to use his hands as an expression of the memories of his brain, you will always give to nature, that is to say, what is outside of you, the character of the lens through which you see it — which is yourself.

Have no fear, therefore, as I say; perhaps of all moments for indulgence in the belief of absolute representation there is none better than our first beginnings.

We might perhaps take an example of the manner in which the truth of a scene in nature affects an artist, and see if from this example we might not deduce a scheme of teaching, perhaps not very deep, perhaps limited at once in its applications, but quite comprehensible in all its parts as one went along. By the use of examples, and by appealing to your own experience, limited as it may be, by taking the facts one by one, we might, if I may so say, get our *theory* along with our *facts*. There is a passage in Fromentin's book on the Algerian Sahel in which are developed various ways of looking at a given scene, so that we can see the picture of it become one thing or another, according to the character or the intentions of the artist.

I shall begin by quoting a part of what he says; and I shall then trust to giving you sufficiently the analogies that he makes, without confining myself to a quotation, which perhaps in this case would be too beautiful to modify, and would not allow me to make the small divisions which should cause it to fit more completely into our argument.

This is the way in which he comes to make this analysis: he was trying to show his friend the geologist, and to explain to him at length, how different painters might look at the scene they had now before them. He begins:

"We were at that moment in the market-place of Blidah. A number of children were playing ball in a way which is cosmopolitan — which is known in the West as well as in the East. A ball or a stick, no matter what it is like, is thrown rapidly and far away. Each player has a stick, and he who gets there first strikes the ball and drives it again. The players were young children from eight to twelve years old, with agreeable faces and delicate bodies, as have most little Moors; with clear-cut features, large and handsome eyes, and skin as pure as that of women. Their arms were naked and their delicate necks shone above their open waistcoats. Their floating trousers were pulled

up above the knee, so as to let them run easily,
and little red *chachia*, like the skull-caps of choir-
boys, just covered the top of the little bald
heads.   Each time that the ball was struck and
started, all together ran in its pursuit, side by
side, in a serried troop, like so many gazelles.
They ran with many gestures, losing their head-
dresses, losing their belts, flying directly to the
goal, and appearing not to touch the earth; for
all that one could see of the light step of the
runners was their naked heels moving in a wave
of dust; and this aerial cloud seemed to hasten
their running and to carry them.

"It was two o'clock; the market was just over,
and the place was entirely deserted, — a square
of houses, low and without roofs; one or two
cypresses pointing above the terraces; the mountain beyond, whose serrate horizon divided the
sky by more than half; that sky empty; a great
stretch of level ground, — that was the landscape.
The houses were of a dead white, slightly dis-
coloured by blistering; the cypresses were black;
the mountain was frankly green; the sky of a

vivid blue, and the earth dust-colour — that is to say, nearly lilac. A single shadow in the middle of the bright light was drawn on that side of the place to which the sun inclined; and this shadow, inundated by reflections from the sky, could have been, in a way, expressed by blue."

"Do you see," said Fromentin to his friend, "this place and these children? The scene is a familiar one, quite in the conditions of what we call *genre*. The frame of the scene, that is to say, the place where it occurs, has this double advantage of accompanying it in a very simple way and still a very local one. The example is as good as any other, and the Orient, which I am trying to represent, can be said to be contained within this narrow frame."

Then he goes on and asks naturally, just as I would ask myself in painting, not by words, but in intention — just as I would ask you in words, if I were giving you a lesson, "What do we see and how shall we look at this subject before us? Are these children who are playing in the sunlight, or is it a place in the sunlight

in which children are playing ?" At once, as
you will see, if you call to mind what Fromentin
has been describing — the scene before him and
his friend could be looked at from two very
different points of view. In the first case, if
we suppose that we are looking at children
playing in the sun, we have a figure painting,
a picture of figures in which the landscape is
accessory. In the second case, if this be a
place in the sun in which children are playing,
then we are looking at a landscape where the
human figure is subordinated — put into a background of intention. Now then, the landscap-
ist will see there, in one case, a landscape;
the figure-painter, in the other case, what he
calls a subject. And in these divisions behold
how many directions open! Will the landscape
painter see it as a scene of colour and of values?
Will he look rather upon the firm lines and
the solitariness of this empty place abandoned to
the noonday sun ? Where will he take — at
what point of their career will he take the little
figures which are scattered over it? Are they

leaving it? Are they entering it? Do they fill the centre? Are they gathered in bunches or divided into spots of colour and moving shape? Is it their mass casting shadows, or the manner in which the reflection of the light breaks up all other details, which most affects him? Will they repeat, in some way or other, the lights and shadows of the entire scene, or will the scene with the greens and blues be modified by the little spots and accents within this frame of landscape? Shall he fix his eye on that solitary cypress and its dark shadow lying upon the blazing earth, thereby making, as you have seen in Fortuny's sketches, of the blue sky above, a half-dulled curtain of blue light? On the contrary, shall that blue light on which he fixes not only the focus of his eye but the direction of his attention — shall that blue light be the subject, and shall he follow its gradations and its variations, through the landscape itself, through the harsh brightness of the houses and their accidental shadows, and finally detect its tones even in the many colours of the children's garments and the

brightest spots of vermilion of their little moving caps?

If he is fond of the angles and sudden contrasts
of line presented by the buildings before him, will
he look upon them as his theme; upon the mountains and the sky as something to reinforce them
and make them harsher and firmer; and find in
the little figures of the children merely something
to keep these lines steadier and more immovable,
by a suggestion of constant change elsewhere?

I have only mentioned a few of the many possi-
bilities that we can derive from this first statement and division of the subject by Fromentin.
Now let us suppose a figure painter, to whom the
landscape will be subordinate in greater or less
degree. Will he use that landscape as a faint
tapestry behind his figures? Will he depend
upon it, on the contrary, to accentuate by strong
lights, and by occasional strong shadows, the
grouping of his children? Will he care for the
mass of their gestures or for their individual succession? Will he make a point of their gestures
and their relation one to the other? Will he

follow out their characters, the characters of their faces, the amusing variety of their costumes? Will he make a symphony of the arrangement of their colours? Will he make a symphony of the lights they scatter, or a pattern of the shadows they cast, which divide or which connect them?

Now from how far will he see them? "For," says Fromentin, "according to whether they are placed near or far, these children will become all or will be nothing. And if you suppose them near enough to the painter, so that the portrait of each one has a dominant interest, then a singular change will appear, and in this very simple picture all the landscape will disappear at once; only something like earth struck by light, from which even the indication of Oriental scenery can be suppressed, will remain."

"Therefore," he goes on, "nothing will remain visible and formulated but a group, important especially by its human significance, composed of children animated by rapid movement and passionate joy, and presented to us so as to draw attention to the expression of gesture with some, and to the play of the faces with others. From elimination to elimination we shall arrive at the reducing of the frame, then at its suppression; then at increasing the group in importance, and then at simplifying it. The costume itself becomes a secondary accident, in a subject whose interest is centred so completely in human forms and expressions."

And then he adds a most important observation : "We can suppress the sun and the excessive light, — a double obstacle which has rarely before to-day preoccupied any mind when the interest was first that of painting human beings."

"What then becomes of the place in which we saw the scene, — this white place, these green cypresses, this white sun of the meridian hours? What becomes of all these outside matters so local and significant; essential if we wish to localize the scene; useless, on the contrary, if we wish to generalize it?"

"Thus we touch abstractions, and without intending it, by the simple fact of a point of view severer and more concentric, we leave outside nature to enter into the combinations of the studio. We abandon thereby relative truth for an order of larger truth, less precise and therefore more absolute, since it is less local."

"For us, at this instant, this little place of Blidah, solitary, violently lit by the full light of a beautiful summer day, these red jackets and white trousers, these pretty children, seem strange to us; and that especially is what pleases us at this moment; this heat, this noise, the diversity of the scene, changing at every moment, — all this composes a unity of multiple impressions, and charms us, and especially so because we see in it the individual character of a picture of the East."

"There are, on the contrary, painters, and I know them, who would only take from this what is necessary, esteeming that what is most interesting in these children is not to be little children of Blidah, but to be children; and these certainly would be in the right."

Let us consider now that for all these varieties of manners of *looking* at this same subject there must be a corresponding system of painting: that the vibration of light, the refraction from the brilliant surfaces described in the Oriental scene just sketched, will demand a placing together of high-keyed colours in painting, in contradiction of another manner that might accentuate, by clearness and little modulation, the sharp and distinct features of the real picture in nature. And which side of nature shall we choose; the look of great breadth and simplicity and absorption of details, or, on the contrary, that appearance of absolute finish and particularity in multitudinousness which almost makes us hopeless of any due record?

The sparkle obtained by Fortuny through constant oppositions; the blending of colour and tone by Delacroix, would again belong to some variety of manner of looking at the subject — in the one the search for smaller things, in the latter for greater ones. And so on, for varieties as many as you can remember painters, — and I abstain from even thinking of draughtsmen. And for each new method of painting, some still more physical, more manual distinctions; thickness or lightness of colour, softening and blending of paint, or bringing its edges harshly together; surfaces with many underneaths, made of many veilings; or with coverings of colour, placed as nearly as possible by the first touch of the brush.

Even the brush would vary; and this mention of the type of our art brings his lengthy statement of differences to an end.

And yet each man would have been true to that nature which we see, and which for us painters only assumes existence in ourselves,—is merely the recall of innumerable memories of sight.

LECTURE III

SUGGESTION AND INTENTION

SYNOPSIS OF LECTURE III.

The illusion suggested by the artist's work is directed by him but mostly made by us. — Selection of one factor in the scene to the exclusion of others. — Drawing a natural convention, a manner of synthesis and suggestion by lines that imply things. — Illusions of black and white. — Hieroglyphics of representation by drawing, a bridge over which we pass to receive the desired impression. — What is there is what we intend to see. — The religious painter : Michael Angelo's view.

LECTURE III.

SUGGESTION AND INTENTION.

In our last lecture we considered at some length how the artist beholds the intentions of his mind reflected in the face of nature; and we took one single example, which we supposed had really happened, of two travellers — one of them a painter — looking at a certain scene in a foreign country, and we considered from how many different mental points of view they could have seen that landscape. We passed on to various other sights enclosed within that same scene, which apparently had not at that time appeared to the mind of the man who had first recorded it; and in the lightest manner we considered a few of these many facets of a described fact.

I believe that I implied that the possible variations would be endless, depending on the combi-

nation of the desires of the artist with certain
sights out of the multitude of things seen; and
that these two great divisions, each one compris-
ing innumerable variations, would be modified
again by unconscious desires, the result of hereditary memories or memories of training. For each
variation there ought to be some special translation by the hand, to which variation by the hand
ought to answer some modification in the use of
materials. For it would be absurd to think that
our practice should be the rule to *determine* our
intentions. And I beg you to remember — you
who are students — to remember to distinguish in
your mind principles which are taught you from
practice which is recommended. But our structure is so complicated, and in our art the relation
of the mind to the matter of the body and to the
matter which the body acts upon, is so subtle, and
varies so much through the indeterminable value
of personality, that we are everywhere met by
what might at first appear contradictions. Some
of these may be insoluble; for many, as we go
along, we shall find, I believe, quite adequate

explanations in the past, in the acquired memories of the artist.

The very manner in which my mind travels away from the direct line of my general intention of speaking to you, warns me of the impossibility of an adequate, or even a plausible consideration of the details involved in the choice that we artists make when we determine or are compelled without self-consciousness to see a scene in some given manner. But with a possible example of contradiction, I may continue by a return to the more direct line of observation.

You will remember that I have only spoken of an entire scene ; I have not supposed the selection of any one factor in the scene, to the absolute exclusion of all others. The art of painting as it has become — as it may perhaps have been in works of the past, lost to us in everything but name — is a manner of representing the entire thing seen as it is translated to us, to our working mind, by colour and light.

I am only speaking of painting as we painters think of it. We go so far as to arrange, as to condense, as to simplify, as to see, under different angles, from different points of perspective; but as painters, properly so, strictly so, we consider ourselves as attempting to embody all that we see. This strict division, which is of the most absolute importance in thinking correctly upon the subject, we shall keep to and consider many times in the course of these talks, and at all times in the direct, practical teaching that I give you.

When I first thought of an exception to the manner in which the artist makes his material plastic, and in an exception was reminded how his material turns against him, I was thinking of that line which divides painting properly from other methods of representation. This is the memory that awoke in my mind as I thought of what we call *drawing*. Three years ago this month I was in a little island in the middle of the Pacific, and I sat through the long afternoon, with a little savage maiden dressed in flowers and leaves, and watched the play of her still younger brothers and sisters. They amused themselves by drawing, in the wet sand of the beach before us, with their fingers, or with bits of broken cane or palm, the outlines of well-known fish and birds; somewhat proud of their skill, and anxious that the stranger should recognize it.   The island dove, the parrot fish, the mullet and the shark, were given by a few lines of remarkable character.   I marvelled at the fact that the savage — the beginner in thinking — was representing these things chosen out by him, in the most abstract conceivable form.   The savage child began artistic life by summing up his acquaintance of sight concerning these creatures into three or four conventional lines — I say conventional, meaning thereby not a single real line, but a line so comprehensive as to include others, the detection of which others had given him this one that he had made.   I might also use the word conventional because, had I not seen these animals, I might not have recognized them as represented by so few characteristics.

Of course, like yourselves, I knew what drawing is, and I had a clear idea of it not different from what I have to-day; but the little lesson

given to me in this way, by the small savage,
brought to my mind the fact that he had begun
first by making a complete synthesis of certain
points that interested him, and that he had
assumed to himself and to others that this synthesis — which was not a copy of nature — this
arrangement and co-ordination of certain facts of
sight, would be understood by others and represent the thing seen.

I need not say, perhaps, that I never supposed
that my individual savage had any conception of
the mechanism of his thought, or would even be
capable of making any analysis of it; but that
we can do.

Now for the exception, that I may get rid of it.
When, in compliment of these children's skill, I
gave them my notebook of smooth paper and
easy-going pencil, to trace again these same forms
in the same way, the lines they traced were no
longer so expressive; their hands seemed to be
checked by difficulties. Apparently the opposition given or made by the material of the sand —
its friction against a motion of the hand, helped

to determine security and certainty of direction of the lines they had traced. As, in another way, the Japanese child who draws a shape beautifully with a brush, has this rendering altered into dryness and apparent irresolution when he uses a lead pencil — an unaccustomed implement. Here again is the artist dictated to by his technique.

As I have said, this is a little exception — a little contradiction, which I think can be easily explained when we ascertain or consider later the involuntary element in the action of the hand.

What is astonishing is that the symbolical character of an outline drawing, — the apparent necessity for a great effort towards condensation that it seems to require, its being in reality the representation of nature which is furthest removed from our actual sight, — that this synthesis should not belong exclusively to late forms of art, to degrees of culture when taste has been refined to the point of appreciating the abstract delicacy of such a mode of representation. On the contrary, you see, it is the

mode of art of the savage; it is the mode of
art that children understand and first care for.
Conventional art, which one would think ought
to repel them, is, on the contrary, the most
suggestive and the most delightful. It must
then be that in a narrower way, the entire
mind of the child or the savage goes into the
object to be represented; and that at once
the main power which we have of accepting
the illusions created by ourselves or others, is the
means trusted to by man in his first attempts.

It is evident that to fill in the empty spaces
of such representations, our imagination is drawn
upon, and thus to a certain extent it is our
imagination that gives to this naked space, separated from the rest of space by a more or less
continuous mark, those details that are wanting
both in colour and in modelling.

You may remember how Lionardo recommends
to the student to look for help in composition to
the spottings and veinings of marble, the breaks
and disintegration of old walls. Therein are to
be found the form of landscapes, of mountains,

and of buildings, and "whatever you are seeking to find."

I have not the passage at hand, and I cannot remember the quaint details of its language. And it is as he says; you have probably discovered these images yourselves, as you have seen dissolving views in the glow of the coals; and you have also, in looking at the glittering points of the stars of heaven, joined them together by lines which make traceable figures; you have gathered the constellations in the net of a geometry.

These arrangements, which are the seeking in the sky for what the artist calls the lines of *composition*, in his little records of pictures — these triangles, these squares — you have really seen them. You, as it were, see the object within an interior sight, and other things that could be seen are dropped away by your will.

Thus, through the crossing of many drawings and tracings, one upon the other, we can choose the one we like. We distinguish and see nothing but the lines of writing that we are looking for, in those crossed letters which in former days we received so frequently. If the words are very important to us, we see none but those, and not the ones that cross them, however distinctly these may all be traced. That is to say, that voluntarily and by effort we strengthen the sensation we wish to have, and weaken the one that we do not care for. And so in looking for a set of composition lines, like those that make the constellation of the Dipper (Great Bear), I end by knowing them as if they had an objective existence outside of me. I may seek out, in the coloured ornamentation of a tapestry, all the curves and leafage which are of a certain colour. They seem to me the pattern, and the remainder a ground upon which they appear, and I may reverse them and so forth.

Thus, if on a white surface I trace two concentric circles, I can look upon the image as representing two black rings, and I shall see black rings; or I can look at the interval between the circles, and see a white ring; and if I turn away, I can still keep my intention, and see the one I choose again, according to my chosen memory.

This very humble illustration is thus akin to the splendid spectacles that are written in the clouds of sunset; and in the same way, we see, on a little piece of paper upon which Rembrandt has scratched a few lines, some vast horizon of open plain, masses of trees, or whatever he has wished us to see with him, so long as he can appeal to our memories of things seen.

This hieroglyph has evoked in us certain images of memory: and still more strangely, a single line has given us the idea of a solid body, —which our eyes see, in what we call reality, as a surface of at least two dimensions.

Let us grant — and it is not certain — that this line reproduces or copies the outline of the object. The difficulty does not decrease; in our

general use of the eyes, just what we notice least
is this outline of objects. What we apprehend
of anything is its full spread, which is always
a coloured surface having a given form,— a
modelled pattern, not an outline.

So that the line of the draughtsman is not
the thing he wishes me to look at. He makes
it to determine the shape of the object, which I,
as it were, cut out by imagination from the white
surface of the paper. What he means me to see
is the interior, within his line. I can follow his
line, but then I cease to see the thing as he
represents it : if my imagination fixes on the
manner in which he has represented the thing,
the outline is but a shadow on the edge. This
is so true, in our usual way of looking at drawings with little but outline, that when the line
is thicker, we feel an intention of representation of shadow ; and any inaccuracy, any want
of sensitiveness in such a use of the outline,
annoys us like a gross blemish. Compare the
line trembling with meaning of Raphael or
Lionardo, now light, now heavy, now wide, now

narrow, though apparently struck out at a single blow — with the stupid intentions of shadowing in the outlines of the outline engravings of the beginning and middle of this century. Compare Blake's outlines after Flaxman with those of weaker, conventional and proper copyists.

In such a case we decide that the increased width of dark belongs to the figure represented. We do this by our own will, which has been started on its path by the intention or will of the artist. If, indeed, he has made a mistake, however brutal, and he meets it fairly, — recognizing it, and leaving the blotch of a patch; — our mind joins with his, and we take the edge of the line that belongs to the figure as the one he must have meant.

Thus, as the line is only meant to separate — meant to divide the figure represented from its background, say of white paper; as it is an abstraction, we shall feel the need of *destroying* it when we come to paint fully. The more full and abundant the details, the richer in modelling, in colour, in light and shade, the more the per-

sistence of the arbitrary outline annoys us.   We
allow it only when the painting is imperfect, flat,
conventional, unreal — in other words, when something is wanting which we replace by a convention.   We see the fact at its worst in the poorer
kinds of what is called artistic stained glass,
where the lead outlines stand out unbidden,
unconnected.[1]

[1] You will remember that this persistence of the outline, of the
abstraction, remains in certain artistic works of high type; for instance, in the fine or mediocre Greek vases — in the first paintings of the
modern period — in most of the Florentine — the most exquisite ones
— and even somewhat in Michael Angelo's great frescoes.   We see its
maintenance and assertion in old Japanese and Chinese art — in such
examples, for instance, as those lately shown in the Museum at Boston.   But there of course, as in several of the cases just referred to,
the *line* is more abstract yet than the mere outline serving to give
the place, and it is used as a special refinement — a sort of orches-
tral accompaniment, which holds the looser details in a firm net of
harmonious arrangement.

The dignity of abstraction, of synthetic choice, of refined abstention, is so evident, that a judicious imitation of it has always been
in favour, and hence the continual tendency to attribute meaning to
the works of art which insist on a prominence of this feature of line
or outline.   It is sometimes put in anyhow rather than it should be
wanting or not very visible; and even incorrect as it usually is —
except in great cases, — it is an appeal to culture, on which many
artists and many schools have lived.

And if you will reflect a little, you will see why the Frenchmen of
the eighteenth century, with the insistence of the line in their Tragedy,

All that the draughtsman, in such a matter as rendering by outlines can give, is the separation of a figure from the background. It is we who endow it with life and resemblance. It is our knowledge of the play of features that makes us see the movement of expression in a couple of lines of a caricaturist, and recognize a likeness in some few characteristics put together.

Yes, it is all very simple: a line or two on the paper, and the spectator sees his friend, or a great landscape is spread for him; the glories of sea and sky; the expression of feeling and of passion, the cadences of action. Yes, that would be easy, if any one could see in it whatever he chose to. But the decision of the creator of the drawing is final. The variety of dreamland into which we enter depends on his manner of opening the gate. And the less he does, or rather appears to do, the more effort is required for all that we have to do. We scarcely wonder at

found it impossible to care for Shakespeare, in whose works the line is covered up — or rather they found him (and they were relatively right, as you will see) too natural — recording too truly the varied aspect of nature, which has no outlines set.

it, and it is only in certain greater cases that
we recognize, through our uplifting and exhilara-
tion, how grand that simple effort may be.

Thus, again, it is the intention of the artist,
not his adequate copying, that makes us understand him. And the larger his intention, the
more he includes, the less he actually gives,
the more we feel the magic of the wand —
his pencil, his graver, his brush-point full of
India ink.

And this magic will continue when, assuming
to use more than line, he gives us effects of
light and shade, and fills in the spaces of outline that divide his paper, with gradations of
light and dark, which may mean as he wishes,
— and as we are persuaded; that is to say,
modellings of form, shadows or sunshine, spottings and deviations of colour or of light.

The surface of the paper may be dusty with
charcoal or crayon — greasy with printer's black
— we see other things than those upon the level
of the paper.

Nay, he may have drawn in white upon a

black ground, as when he draws upon a slate; and we sympathize with the struggle; — the white marks which indicate how black the hair; how deep the red of the lips.

If his drawing be on grey paper, we can see the light tone of the light and follow its variations. Has he not made us believe that wherever he has *not* put dark the place is to be called light, — the glitter of metal, the glow of the sky, the shine of the sunlight? He may care more for the light and dark which to us mean form, and he may abstract for the thing he wishes to represent certain details, as those of form, and abandon all representation of the full look of nature. That is to say, he may be what the French call a *dessinateur*, — an exclusive lover of line or form. Or he may propose to himself, with Rembrandt, a synopsis of everything that the eye can take in, — colour and light and shade, form and the movement of form, and the peculiar tone which envelops each picture that we make in looking at nature.

For each separately and all together of these results, he may make lines and spots upon a ground of white. Their joining or their separation will make, at the distance from the drawing that we assume, a tint which means to us the tint of nature. The cross lines and cross hatchings of an engraving rush together at a certain distance, and the eye feels in them a continued impression of tint darker or lighter as the marks are nearer or further apart.

Even if our eye sees that this fusion is imperfect, we know so well what is meant that we are not troubled by the drawing of shadow in a head of Lionardo, for instance, through a number of parallel straight lines, put not closely together. We see those lines not as lines but as one shadow. And you follow, in the same way, the intention of the line engraver, when his curves describe the shape of what he wishes. You know that a woman's arm is not covered with curved stripes; you know that the human face is not tattooed with fine lines fitting its form. But you recognize the intention. The lines are the section, apparently, of the place where they are put; and this accumulation of sections, if correct, reassures you as to your pursuit of the form in the engraving.

So that we follow, indeed, only the mind of the artist. When he leaves this system of lines, which describes form as a soft bracelet describes the shape of the arm of a woman, and when he suddenly adopts a new system of lines to mark that he is not thinking of form but of shadow, we follow him again into another form of artifice, and see as he wishes. In the differing arrangement of lines or spots, he may now give us the impression of texture, now the impression of the tint he wishes to represent.

If he has a given quantity of white and of black, the effect will be much less, when he rubs them together and makes a grey, than when he leaves the same quantity of white and black side by side, and makes them affect the eye and excite it by contrast. In such a case he may place them together, without mixing, in innu-

merable combinations; each arrangement, as in
the art of the wood engraver, will give a separate tint, and their greatest amount of black will
even yet be transparent, because it will be permeated by the lustre of some separate little
white spots and lines.

This, by the bye, is one of the systems used
by some of the latest modern painters, — im-
pressionists, *pointillistes*, etc. Photographed for
that purpose, their placing of colour side by side
resembles the mechanism of engraving on wood,
which may have given the first idea. In this
case, as in the case of the little checker patterns,
the little rain of dots of the wood engraver,
our eye is first excited by one colour, then
calmed by another; in the painting by a contrast of colour, in the engraving by contrast of
light and dark. The energies of nature, therefore, — not their realities, — are translated by
our own energies.[1]

The process, which is extremely interesting

---

[1] Indecisions of seeing — our not seeing all with equal distinctness,
which is part of our sight as well as seeing distinctly — are recalled
also by such methods.

from the indefinite extension it can receive, is the one we see in stuffs and brocades. The Japanese silks and brocades and common cotton goods offer us an endless series of wonderful solutions of the problem, where the colour resulting from these dissociations of values makes a bloom difficult to render into words by name, extremely difficult to render by colour of one homogeneous mixture. And indeed we can see those effects given in this singular manner by the patterns especially used for men's clothes, in which ever so many "shades," as they are called, of grey, are produced by the placing of alternate spots or stripes of black and white, which only mix *in the eye,* and get their definite existence there. These humble methods of the men who make the patterns of your trousers are, in another very complicated way, the methods through which Rembrandt has awakened your appreciation of light and dark. Those scratches of different sizes; those blotches of white, more or less stained; those lines, now blurred, now sharp, have allowed him to make, on a bit of paper, pictures as wonderful as any painting ever painted; as full of reality, of mystery, of imagination, of intensity of natural and supernatural life as his stupendous paintings themselves.

It is always hard to pass from what delights us, but wherever, as we have decided in our first considerations, wherever any full method, any adequate clothing created by the artist for his ideas, has resulted from his using all his powers, there has been a mockery made by others, an imitation of the methods, a copying of the outside clothing. Now curiously enough, just here, we can again recall in our first classification of imitation, of a manner of looking at nature as if she were petrified and crystallized, in some shape far from her fluid readiness to change; far from her being seen by us only through colour and light ever varying.

In certain etchings, for instance, we can see quite distinctly what is obscurely hinted at through many works of art of different processes of execution. Many times we see in work that we feel is poorer, the etching of an etching, if I may so say, the rendering into black and white of a nature — for anything outside us is nature — all in black and white, which nature is created for the purpose in the inferior artist's mind. For the glories of nature in which we lose ourselves are not the glories of black and white abstraction. The spaces that we see are seen by us as coloured light (if I may so put it), and he whom we call the painter, most of all artists, emphasizes his recognition of this luminous coloured impression under which all things are seen. It matters not, though it be not clear at first, that he has used only black and white ; in any case when he has wished to give the sensation of nature, he has made a synthesis of this luminous impression, which in some way bears out the suggestion of something more than black and white being copied in his representation. Never has he or any artist of full life copied or represented the representation. I have named the etcher as most evident in such a failure, most tiresome in his copying the look of an etching — not the look of *things* that etching fairly conveys.

So the water-colourist imitates a water colour,
and the oil-painter the look of what I have been
told was a real hand-painted oil colour. The surface, the contexture of some kind of work of art
is in their minds. Many a painter of the beginning of the century saw Roman statues when he
looked at his model. Indeed it might be said
that he even saw his model in the form of a
plaster casting. Only the strong obsession of
another individuality in nature, and the influence
of earlier studies, forced him occasionally, as
with David when painting portraits, into a pursuit of the luminous and intimate changes which
are impossible out of the moving flesh and blood.
Remember now that I am only speaking in a
general way, and that each case has its own
record. Because again, extreme and delicate
beauty can be obtained even in such artificial
arrangements. But they need a man behind them,
and he must make an attempt to conciliate them
with what he feels of all nature. Thus in Prud-
hon's lovely work, the " plaster-cast " shadows
look no longer like an admiration of the statue,

but become certain types of beauties of shade, such as are felt by us in the mysterious destruction of colour values by moonlight.

And there are even sculptors who have managed to give you an impression that the originals they pursued in imitation were already cast in plaster.[1]

We have passed already too far away from the first question of the rendering of many things by a single one, of the suggestion of things that are not there. Any artist who has kept many studies of his own will remember the manner in which we select out of some drawing certain lines, certain marks, — because it may be a drawing having more or less colour added to it or shade. We select out of the marks on the paper certain ones which bring back, by connection with memory, the entire picture which we saw at the time that we made it; whether those lines were records of nature or records of the imagination — that is to say, of the intention of doing something. It

---

[1] Even in Japanese lacquers you can distinguish those which represent nature in gold or black varnish from those which represent well-executed lacquer patterns.

might be even such a question as the indication of
a whole subject by the supposed main lines representing movement, which movement fully carried
out in all its details, and placed in what might be
called a body, was to make, by a process of evolu-
tion, a completed work of art.

Last Wednesday Mr. Cazin was reminding me
of the danger of looking over former notes and
studies when out of them some one had to be
found which we needed at once; the tendency,
as one came across each special record, to see an
entire scene — either a scene in nature or a scene
that had occurred in our mind, in which, delighted
with the delight of former memories, we rebuilt
the entire world of former experience, and forgot
at each time that on some other piece of paper, on
some other sheet of an album, was the one little
dry separate fact that we had wished to consult.
And he added: "I sometimes do not care to look
over them myself; I find some friend — some one
in the family, who is willing to hunt out the
special thing; because he has no other association
than that of the moment."

Who shall fathom the mystery of the impressions made by art — impressions which become
confused, when one tries to declare them and
describe them; strong and clear if we feel them
again, even by the recall of memory; so that we
realize how much of ourselves constituted the
feelings that seemed to come out of the things
that struck us. In our art these impressions are
tangible, if I may say so. We enjoy what we
think is the representation of the certain things, at
the same time that some sense of what they mean
for our mind affects and moves us. These figures,
these objects, which seem to be the thing itself to
a certain part of our intelligence, make a sort of
bridge over which we pass to reach that mysterious impression which is represented by form as a
sort of hieroglyph; a speaking, living hieroglyph,
not such a one as is replaced by a few characters
of writing; in our art and in that sense a sublime
means and creation of man, if we compare it to
that in which thought can reach us only through
conventional arrangements of the signs we call
letters. An art more complicated certainly than

literature, but infinitely more expressive, since, independently of the idea, its sign, its living hieroglyph, fills the soul of the painter with the splendour that things give ; their beauty, their contrast, their harmony, their colours, — all the undivided order of the external universe.[1]

Later, we may consider, if we have time, the enormous difference between the representation, even incomplete, through the thing itself, and the representation by a name for it.

Should you hesitate a moment, and believe — or rather imagine — that the reasons I give are subtle, are fine-drawn, pause a moment and ask yourselves, on the contrary, whether they are not gross, heavy attempts at handling with words a thing so subtle even as the representation of anything by a line. If, in fact, I can express these ideas adequately in words of ordinary language, I must have left a great deal unexplained. Art begins where language ceases, and the impressions that we receive, and the manners through which we render them, are in themselves so subtle that

[1] Paraphrased from Delacroix.

no one yet has been able to analyze more than a certain exterior or part of the mechanism of sensation and of representation. I have said art — I mean of course *our* arts, painting, sculpture, architecture, music.

Do not let us talk of our putting down — recording — what was there; there was there what we intended to see. The religious feeling of the religious painters of the past had no other means of expression than the faces of the people they saw about them. The women living then, whose faces are enshrined for us in the pictures of Christian sanctity, were not different from those of to-day. They had the same lightness of mind, the same caring for fashion, the same meannesses, the same devotion, the same high pure-mindedness, that they have to-day. From what they showed, the artist who cared for the higher things chose what he cared for. He who did not *see*, as we say — that is to say, who did not *mean*, — gave us dryness, hardness and meanness of character in the early portraits of those same periods when religious art flourished.

My students, perhaps, have never read the journal of the painter, Francis of Holland, who went to Rome, and knew Vittoria Colonna, and through her kindness managed to meet Michael Angelo, and to record a few expressions of his. They may remember Francis's portrait of the glorious old gentleman, a demigod of art, with his collar up, with his hat pulled down, and the gloves he wore to protect his age : the Michael Angelo who at that time passed through the streets of Rome to make his calls. It is years since I saw the journal of Francis of Holland : and I quote from a long memory. But something like this was said in the cool chapel of the closed church of San Silvestro in Monte Cavallo — in answer to the questions they asked : " Of what consisted elevation in painting : is it the representation of great and splendid things, of angels and saints — and robes and backgrounds of gold ? "

" Good painting," said Michael Angelo, " is noble and devout in itself, for with the wise nothing elevates more the soul and turns it toward devotion than the difficulty of perfection, which is a tendency to approach God and to be united to Him ; for good painting is as a copy of His perfections, a shadow of His brush, a music, a melody.

"The painting of which I speak, and which I praise, asks only the imitation of one of the innumerable things which God's Infinite Wisdom has created, — be it [a fish of the market-place or] a bird of the air."

The heavy record of Francis of Holland runs somewhat like this : but out of much tedious misrendering, speaks the real voice of the man whose poetry in verse expresses an anxious sense of the spiritual world. If we only see that painting, in the words of Delacroix, another very great artist, requires the whole man ("veut son homme tout entier"), this humble dedication of Michael Angelo's powers need not surprise us.

As the creature represents in itself a record of the forces that have made it and made also the world, and as it is in so far an epitome of the universe, so the man who brings his mind to contemplate the creature, is himself communicating

with the entire world.   He is acting in the spirit
of poetry, which touches us by establishing, over
and over again, this connection of ourselves with
the universe ; through our seeing how, in the
poet's mind, some single thought, sometimes some
mere fancy, some mere word, has ties with all
that we care for most, with the very foundations
upon which we live.

LECTURE IV

MISAPPREHENSIONS OF MEANING

SYNOPSIS OF LECTURE IV.

What we see in an artist's representation is our sight of our memories in it. — This not equally possible for all. — Ignorance or oppressive knowledge may interfere. — Difficulties that may stand in the way of appreciation. — Difficulties in the way of the painter's free sight owing to training. — The artist's frequent narrowness not unnatural. — Often it is the proof of a final closing of his susceptibility. — Reasons for not enjoying certain works of art. — The student may add to his powers from what is furthest away from him in art. — Of necessity the artist's own record of memories may come to be understood only as other people's memories accumulate, if he goes beyond what all expect. — Hence time must be a factor in the growth of appreciation.

LECTURE IV.

MISAPPREHENSIONS OF MEANING.

WE shall have seen, then, that the illusion suggested by the artist's work is directed by him, but mostly made by us; that we no longer see his mere piece of canvas, when he tells us that it is a hollow mirror of the world; that the marks he makes upon the piece of grey or white paper become to us memories of what we have seen or desired to see; and that, though I know that this is Naples yellow, that that is cobalt, that I can name each colour and each mixture of colour, in the five-minute sketch that Turner puts on a bit of Whatman, I can at the same time that I see them all separately, the paper, the kind of colour, the paint and brush-mark, see also the blue Mediterranean basking in the southern sun.

We have looked a little way into the mystery
implied in those scratches that the savage, or a
Rembrandt, makes, — and we saw in what is
called drawing a natural convention, a manner
of synthesis and suggestion; in it man speaks
to man by lines that imply things. And we can
think of these as a bridge over which our spirit
passes, beyond these things implied, to reach still
further, to newer sights, or to some meaning
more or less recognized by us, according to the
intensity of our desire, according to memories
suggested to our view of our relations with
the universe, or what the universe itself may
mean.

Then, in another attempt at limitation, at
definition, I said that art begins where language
ceases; and as I said it, I was reminded again
of the wider and vaguer sense of the word *art*,
which, however, we cannot better.

I thought how the writer, the poet, uses words,
and how their ordinary use and value are changed
by him; how their ordinary position is misplaced,
that he may convey, through his art, an illusion

impossible to the average language, which language is not personal with him.

By his cadences, by the stress laid upon certain words, by his placing of words in an artificial frame, the poet suggests, not the actual thing itself that he says, but what our memories will make of it; as soon as he has thrown us out of the hearing of the language of every day.

A line came back to me, while I read my own words to you, a line of Virgil; a line loved by Millet the painter; remembered by me, perhaps, because of its association with the story of his painting:

"Majoresque cadunt altis de montibus umbrae."

Certainly, the real fact of the shadows gradually filling the plain below the mountains was known to Millet; but when he repeated the line, or *saw* it aloud — if I may so say — he felt how the word "Majores," which means only greater, is placed so as to suggest constantly greater increase; and how the shadows, which end the line in the soft word "umbrae," that means these, have spread from the beginning of the line, and have descended, as if with a fall, from the high mountains.

And again, we said that we saw what we intended to see, we who paint; and Michael Angelo defined for us what made a religious painting, by the spiritual attitude of the painter. Through these followings and pursuit of the fact that each artist sees in his own way, through memories of what he has been, and of what he has liked; even when he says to himself, in assertive moments, that "that is the way the thing looked," we shall come to perceive, perhaps, why it is, that this faceting of truth must be so, — how the perpetual Maia, the illusion and enchantment of appearances, plays for each of us a new part, sings for us a new personal song, — as if she returned our admiration — as if she cared — indeed, as if she existed, in the way that we say we know her; for she takes form in us and fits our shapes.

If, therefore, we cannot separate ourselves from what we see; if our energies are necessary to help the artist to impress us; if what he appeals to us about is not an actual sight, but merely our sight of our memories in it, so that we could not put these things to a man born blind on his first recovery of sight, we know that it is because at least a great part of the influence exerted by the artist is the recall to our own experience of our own memory. We build upon that, and recognizing its conformity with that of the artist's memory, we trust him and continue beyond experience to whatever new sights he may wish to lead us among. But we must believe first in the conformity with our own of these first memories of his which he offers us.

Now this is not equally possible for all; it will depend upon our sensitiveness, our capacities of all kinds.[1] To some kinds of intellect certain con-

---

[1] Sensitiveness — at the word I pause for a moment. Has it ever occurred to you how excusable are the misapprehensions of many literary critics of pictures — such as any of you of my hearers who are artists may have suffered from in yourselves, or in what is still more aggravating, the misjudgment of greater men — all of whom have suffered in that way ? Constable, Gericault, Delacroix, Millet, Rousseau, Manet, Corot, — the list is great.

Just think a moment.

The different arts have each and in common, one property which is *Expression :* based on a correspondence between the sensations of

tradictions to their memories of sight will be so important that those contradictions — the deficiencies of the painter or artist, will prove insurmountable. The reminder of the illusion will not take place with them to a sufficient extent to

the soul and the sensations of the body. A colour, a line, a sound, may influence the soul with a similar sentiment of result. A painting, a statue, a melody, shall cause upon us, the public, a similar moral impression, and the literary critic may translate it for the public by some explanation — say that of *sweetness ;* and that without his being able to understand what is properly sculptural, pictorial or musical in this triple expression. Notes, lines and colours smile or weep, are sad or gay, equally, but each in its way. And yet it is neither sadness nor joy which constitute what is proper to music, to painting or to sculpture.

Thus each art has its particular language and another in common understandable by all. A French poet, whose thought I am following, has compared three arts, painting, sculpture and music, to three persons speaking in three languages, say French, German and Italian, before another who should understand only English. Now there is a common human expression which will allow these three persons to be understood in *part*, but certainly not in all, nor in what is most precise, and in fact only in what each person would consider a mere help to his own language.

The public are like the hearer: because they feel, they therefore think they can judge works, only part of which they are competent to pronounce upon.

There is in each competent artist a sort of unconscious automatic mathematician, who, like the harmonist in music, the colourist in painting, resolves in his way the problem of sight or sound which the scientist puts into an equation.

move the entire mind. It may come from too much ignorance; it may come from too oppressive a knowledge of certain facts. We should be troubled by Shakespeare's geography, by his statements of historic fact, and the characters he

And yet owing to the extreme difficulty of these problems and the improbability of their being solved completely by them, people have the assurance to decide about them.

Perhaps this may be the cause of the special failures of the critic of paintings. Music has been noted. It is not possible to acknowledge that one does not know one note from another, and yet criticise them. But the plastic arts have no complete notations. (Architecture, however, can use some notation.)

These differences are not absolute, but are relative to the limits of our perceptions, which are not the same for sight and sound.

The series of musical sound appears to us discontinued. The gamut could not be figured by the contiguous positions of a point moving on a line. The gamut would be more like the stepping of a pair of compasses on a right line. The series of colours, on the contrary, is continuous. Hence you can see how infinitely more difficult to follow and to place. And also more difficult to find out the man who makes a mistake in criticism of coloured appearances. Hence of course the fact that the painter only can execute his painting: he cannot notate it in colour. And so for the lines, which are born of his personality, their directions imply a number of curves whose radii are in infinite number and are continuously variable. All equations fail before them; at least by the means of scientific analysis of which man yet disposes. And yet we know that they must be obedient to the Sovereign Art and Science which has moulded the world and which has somewhere above us an adequate notation.

To ask, then, of the average critic a sensitiveness capable of such

builds, were we not, fortunately for our appreciation of what he meant, bowed down into the right attitude by the pressure of long continued opinion.

I think that I can remember my professor of anatomy's objection to the Venus of Milo, about whose hips he had much misgiving. Something was wrong there, (and as she is big) with no small measure of blunder. If you have followed your course of anatomy, you will know what I mean and whether the trouble has been removed with the readjustment of the statue. But this defect spoiled the pleasure my teacher might have had. And so with Barye's animals, which my teacher admired freely — it troubled him that certain deformations and exaggerations were there; and

appreciation is cruel. Music and its rules he may hold, because explained and notated. But how is he to hear the Voice of Nature calling to the painter, unless he too has a similar physical sensitiveness ?

For from what we saw a moment ago, when we noticed the subjective continuity of the impressions of colour, and the infinity of line, you can see why nature, the world of the eye, is always singing to the painter. The notes of the prism continue indefinitely, and the painter, or he who has his temperament, sees at every moment in the world about him the absolute harmony which the other arts obtain by effort. That is why the record of nature is the painter's manner of expression.

apparently the result of deliberate purpose with Barye, — the intention, perhaps, which had become a habit, of changing the scale so as to produce the impression of size; as the actual bronze was small, but had to appear the size of life. Had these been the errors of a novice, my professor might have been more indulgent. To his own modelled works my teacher was more indulgent. Their defects being mixed with the qualities he was looking for, he easily allowed for these defects, and could create for himself the necessary illusion.

If there can be all this difference of appreciation in such an art as realistic sculpture — if I may use the term — so near the actual form, so tangible, so much the thing itself that a sculptor can be blind, as you all have seen, and yet make a statue or image whose form at least, if not the appearance of its form, will be correct, — how much more excusable — if I can say so — how much more pardonable, will such deficiencies of sympathy appear to us in those who cannot enjoy the full illusion of painting, of drawing; of the more sublimated manners of art.

Any sort of knowledge (which is stored memory), any memory of training, any kind of *prejudice,* as we may define it, may stand in the way of appreciation.

We shall see the result of a sort of obsession in the intellect, like a hard deposit in a living body, prevent the free action of its energies, and arrest its acquirement of new sympathies. As in our studies and the records of the impression of nature upon us artists, in the things we do before new sights, in the notes we take of what is new to us, we are hampered (fortunately for our self-esteem, without knowing it frequently) by the habits of memory of the studio, by certain methods of painting or drawing (and of sight even, as I have shown you), which were invented and perfected for other sorts of sight and things, seen by others than ourselves, who taught them to us; or seen by ourselves, under conditions far removed in the past. Hence the difficulties of the painter who brings to his study in the open air of the New World — harsh, clear, light-coloured, crystalline — not the principles but the methods he has learned in studios of grey and rainy France, or the dry formulas of school-bred Germany. And if in the face of ever-changing nature, he is overburdened by that part of himself which has hardened like his bones, and he repaints his old likings of studio practice — how excusable is he in objecting to the newer impressions of others: the works of others who are not carrying as a weight the same memories of practice and sight which he has.[1]

[1] This was part of a lesson noted by a pupil.

We have considered the technical sides of art as merely the means of expression. We have noticed, however, that these means — this dress in which the idea is presented to us — are only, in part, the result of the feelings and perceptions of the artist : that he begins at first by accumulating memories that properly are not his own ; that are the memories of his ancestry, of his first predilections, and most decidedly of his first training. Later on — we must always remember that time is of no consequence, and that these words may represent a very brief interval or a very long one — the artist introduces into what he does his own development of personal memories. He may, then, come to a prodigious difficulty, the explanation of which difficulty will give us the clue of certain mistakes which are not infrequent in the work of art, and which especially control its appearance to-day. We can suppose the artist passing out of his childhood of art, out of the pleasant expanse of certain methods and a liking for the manner of looking at the world embodied in these methods. He has become a graver person. He has strong feelings that become more and more

And if these objections to sincere expression, perfectly natural, as I said, belong to a narrow mind, if indeed all this is but another statement of all that I have been noting, either combined with strict views, or joined to a tortuous nature, the main ones in that part of his life that he desires to express. Or else he may always have had such graver or higher or more noble sides, which have remained dormant during the apprenticeship to the external ; and he may revert to these fundamental loves of early life.

Suppose, for instance, that all that turn towards the interior world which we call religion, should awake in him or come back to him from the time when he lived contented, breathing the atmosphere of feeling, out of which he had passed insensibly, into the dryer and more confined air of the average æsthetic life. For you must not think that the average æsthetic manner of life is so much richer than any other. A Bohemian may be a chump like any other fellow. Nor does the love of the ornamental dado or of "art colours" necessarily expand the mind. During those years of apprenticeship, the external body of his art will have been made by something like crystallization. He will have accepted methods that belonged to men of other ways of feeling — methods never used to express any depth of thought or emotion, meant perhaps as an indication of there being really nothing more in the world than the momentary pleasant perceptions through which we pass without looking beneath, or without any interior questioning. What will the artist do ? His language, its cadences, its colouring, every part of it, will have been meant to state something almost the reverse of what he really now feels most. His methods do not imply *respect;* he has learned to express himself only in accents of lightness or triviality, and he knows no others. He can no longer sing in any other tones than those to which he has trained his voice. What shall he do ?

we shall see here, in a sort of natural history of
man, part of the causes of opposition to artists
whose career has been a free one, open to nature's grace and influence as the earth they love
is to the showers and the sun.

If he is a very great man, — I mean, rather, a great personality like
Millet, for instance, — he will live in a struggle with the methods that
he uses.   There may occasionally be such successful cases, which prove
— to what should be our great satisfaction — that the human mind
cannot be classified like the forms of the lower ranges of animal life.

But all the probabilities of life are against the man whom I have
tried to bring up before you.   His means will contradict his end.   We
shall then feel curiosity, interest — anything that you may like to name
except the main thing, and that is that he has expressed *himself*.

This difficulty will not be recognized easily by himself.   He will
wonder why people do not take him seriously.   He will wonder why
his work is always treated as a remarkable piece of technique ; while
he has perhaps often hoped that it might preach something, that it
might at least give testimony or recognize some lesson of doctrine.
As you will remember, when we explained to ourselves how limited
our range of vision was, we saw how difficult it was to free ourselves
from our memories of sight ; we can thus appreciate how the artist's
memories will call up no other memories of sight, in such a case, but
those connected with the expression of ideas which he does not now
care for ; and since he is always sure that he is himself, it will become
almost impossible for him to go against these memories, gauge them
as they are, and put them behind him.   He would have to be born
again.

This, I think, will explain the feeling that we have to-day, of so
much in the art of painting or of sculpture — not to mention the
others — which makes us doubt the existence of strong feeling and

Add to this the temptations of life : the fierce
desire for success and selling one's wares; the
necessity of banding together, and thereby keeping others out — all the things that excuse what
we do collectively that is wrong in the individual; — and the reasons for not admitting as
plausible the illusions of others, become clearer,
and however to be regretted, less unnatural.

desire in the artists whose works are meant to appeal to some of our
feelings. We can see why, in certain German painters, for instance,
the method of painting invented and developed for the representation
of barnyard scenes, of comic situations in peasant-life, for the tawdry
imitation of silks and satins and theatrical show, is anomalous — I
might say unthinkable, when it is applied to the Divine tragedy of
the life of Christ, or to carry the plaint of the exiled sons of Eve.

I have taken the German painter as a better instance, because of
a certain lower level of art developed in Germany, which allows us to
see more distinctly, by not calling upon us to judge the exceptional.
The same analysis would, however, distinctly apply to the methods
of the French artists, learned in the studios of the Beaux-Arts ; where
the point has been to make a good study of the model, with or without drapery, in such a way as to avoid getting into any difficulties,
and to keep entirely within the range of the academic — a range less
annoying, perhaps, than the vulgar, because it appeals to us as people
of society, but just as preposterous in the representation of the ideal.

Or again, the methods used for what is called decoration, for the
covering of surfaces of walls, or stained glass, or any kind of furniture of a more æsthetic pretension — all of which methods, in the
usual way, are meant to escape work, to ease the mind from inquiry,

Besides, it is inevitable that on one side the painter — the artist — will be narrow; I had almost said must be narrow. He has to act; he has to choose here and now; he cannot travel on two paths at once. For the moments in which he brings his idea into the real world

from emotion; to bring back things to the intellectual value of the average carpet. These methods cannot be informed at once by any passion which will take them away from the irresponsibility of the furniture which they match. So that the question put to me by the Philadelphia lady, as to which of the decorative firms had the most religious feeling, seems preposterous.

It is true that sometimes these methods do not annoy us so much, partly for this very reason, that they are so inadequate that we do not hear any voice; partly because, as the methods of decorative art are of necessity connected with the past, and with the firmest foundations of the pictorial art, there is something which at least on that *one* side may seem to connect with what we know has been a part of certain great expressions in the past: as the use to-day of gold in a background, or of a line of gold for the halo around a saint's head, reminds us that once upon a time, there were artists whose works represent all the religious feeling of the ages, and that these artists used gold in their backgrounds, and gold in the halos of their saints.

First, therefore, see that your methods are respectful. Never make light of difficulties or slip easily over what you find to be obstacles. Better be gawky than flippant in your work. Imitate in your methods the methods of religious life, even if they oblige you to the lengthiest preparations. And if a passionate impulse carries you away, your expression will still have the accent that comes of previous respectful meditation.

of mechanics, what he has to *do* is all that he can manage. It cannot be done too thoroughly, too singly. He is like the general, the commander in the field: the battle has to be won; what side issues can there be? The riders trample down their own companions who have fallen; the cannon wheels crush out friend and foe.

From this habit of mind alone, the artist, on the side that he has in common with men of action, may well retain that attitude which marks the soldier in a cause.

"A quoi pensez-vous?" (What do you think of all this?) said Fromentin the painter, to his friend the officer, who was holding, almost by force of will alone, some little far-off post in the desert, just conquered.

"My friend," the officer answered, "if I thought of all this, I should become too much of a philosopher for a soldier."

So also, the artist usually closes his mind to argument; wisely enough, the combination of his instincts reminds him — convinces him of a fact: that his opponent's being able to argue better

than he does, does not prove his opponent to
be in the right; it only proves that his opponent
is stronger in argument. As to himself, he must
be persuaded besides being convinced. And he
cannot, without loss to his power of grasp by
what we call instinct, — or what I have tried to
state is a form of genius, — accustom himself to
go step by step, at the pace of the logicians. So
that he is obstinate, and a dreamer, like many
men of action; and, like them, not so different
from women.

And his moral nature having to be soothed
by a sense of justice, he attributes to those
who give other impressions than his, who build
another kind of bridge, some form of moral
obliquity. A well-known French painter repeats
that if Millet were alive and he could again keep
him from the Salon, he would do so, on account
of his deteriorating influence. Ingres says of
Delacroix, who yet had defended him as an
artist, when Ingres was still misunderstood, "Ne
me parlez pas de cet homme là." (Don't mention
that man to me.) One sees the same sort of

thing in the white men who hold some post in
far-away lands, among what they call natives.
Were they all to understand them, with sympathy, the grasp of the conqueror might be loosened.
It is the power, the awful power for the moment,
of ignorance.

Much of this is the result of knowledge crystallized too rapidly. But knowledge is simply
a filling of part of the great void of ignorance.
The beginner, the youngster, out of school or
still in it, has of course memories that are
fewer; the first associations of some manner of
liking with the thing seen. How can he help
seeing little else than his methods just learned,
and with the faithfulness and "solidarity" of the
boy, look for these only — "the kind of thing
the other fellows are after." Indeed, he hardly
recognizes anything in nature that is newer than
his own records, unless some one has "done it,"
who himself has some actual connection with him,
and over whose method of work he can walk as
on a bridge, to this new land of representation.

He may so crystallize his memories that all

else is closed, and he drops out of the list, at length; or he may go the furthest length of his classmates, and walk as far as they.

As small or great will be the same to him, he may do as David's pupils used to do; throw things at certain pictures, say the famous Watteaux, and object physically. It is not that he *sees* the other thing and objects. He does not see it at all. I have known an intelligent young painter burst out with laughter at the painting of a great Delacroix, not one square inch of which he could have paralleled as mere brush work, in a thousand years of continuous effort; and then go and admire voluptuously the surface of one of the smaller French painters of to-day — the name doesn't matter — a surface he could parallel and reproduce fairly; — all but the invention connected with it, and that freedom of brush which sometimes seems to mean: I have learned this way, but I might have learned another, for I am a good executant.

Like Narcissus, and as fatally, he was admiring his capacities reflected in the smooth mirror of a painter, as a mirror undisturbed by any motion, any waves of the great wind that blows through the world from higher spaces. Probably by this time the water nymphs below have dragged him down.

Again we return to this — that we see in the work of art what we wish to see: the picture of our own memories of sight; the mirror of what we are or have grown.

Now if in the artist (on his poorer side) we have analyzed his resistance to impressions offered to him, at the same time with others that he dislikes, or objects to, or does not understand, what must not be the obstacles in ·the way of people with still less sensitiveness of organization? Not that all artists are more sensitive to art than those who are not artists. Remember that what decides the career of a painter is the curious relation between the eye and the hand — the desire and power of making a movement with the hand, to repeat and recall the memories of the brain.

Do not let us confuse things.

A writer to the savage is a man who writes; a painter is a man who paints. To the savage, any man who can make, as we all do, marks which can be interpreted into sentences, is a writer. Difficult it is to gauge whether he can understand what gradations we see involved in the word. To the savage of savagery, to the savage of civilization, any man is a painter who, making marks with paints, can have them interpreted into the meaning of things.

But we are obliged to supply, by the use of the name of artist, the deficiency in classification. The artist is he who, as I said when I defined art again, effects an intellectual connection with nature outside him; has accumulated memories of sight rarer than the common, and memories of their connections; and is open to new memories placed so suddenly with older ones that they look like first apprehensions and reachings-out.

But what appeal can there be to the man who has few memories of sight that are personal, few acquired through works of art? Museums, collections of various kinds — the looking at nature with the feeling that it can be rendered; the enjoyment of nature on account of art, and of art on account of nature; all this will tend to make a collection of memories and encourage the confidence in them, and prevent their being lost or displaced. For the child has often begun to collect impressions, and yet after a time loses those first memories of the pleasures of sight, as other memories of other things displace the less reasoned, less analyzed early impressions.

We can end by seeing how, still more than with the artists, the great public recognize slowly any new addition to the wealth of the world in the records of things seen, in the works of art that imply such records, be they of painting, of sculpture, or of the smaller arts of decoration, and finally why the mediocre and the plausible must always reign for a time.

Were we to look about any museum, — were we to look about this one, — we should surely see waifs, fragments of work stranded on the shore, if I may say so, — bits of old shipwrecks; but which, at one time, were carried over seas, buoyant and inflated with the wind of popular favour. Museums, alas! are like all great institutions — not merely ideal; they give examples of what should be avoided, of what ultimately is avoided; but which for a moment confuses the mind of the young, and impresses memories upon them, that may return to do them harm — at least automatically.

It is always impossible to explain how such things have happened to be included. Perhaps they have not happened here by themselves, — they are parts and fragments of circumstances not so painful. To obtain and enjoy means for greater purchases, we are willing to accept gifts that we ought to decline; we yield to personal considerations. Have I not recommended persons and paintings myself, rather than claim superiority, — rather than dishearten in the public an interest which has to be fanned like a small ember about to go out?

These examples represent an average perception and reflect average personal likings of a moment; but as soon as something more has been acquired

and expressed, then *we see all there is in them,* and
are shocked at coming to the end of a world;
since it must then be unlike the real one which it
represents; for the real one has always more to
give to our inquiry or appreciation. And yet
even *there,* with certain minds (so true is the definition that *we* make the value of the work of art),
we shall detect their delight in feeling assured
that there is nothing more, that they know every
bit of it, and can name all that is there.

Offensive to them must be the work of art, the
man, the kind of view of any truth, which cannot
easily be held in a short formula, which has any
impression of superiority — and escapes their
grasp.

Some of us dislike, some of us fear, all of us are
at least chary, of what cannot as yet be cata-
logued and stamped with a trade-mark.

Balzac had a motto: "Comprendre c'est par-
donner"; and, to a certain extent, I hope that
this analysis of the reasons for dissenting from
admiration and enjoyment of certain works of
art, will make you, my students, pause a moment

before resenting. Patience — long-suffering, has always been the badge of those really favoured by Minerva; and one of the earliest of great artists in words has shown what she did for Ulysses; and how she brought him home at last, and placed him on the throne that belonged to him.

We may also — we students — as pupils together (for Michael Angelo, you know, went to school, as he called it, when he was so old that he could not see, but had to handle the famous ancient torso he cared for, which goes by his name), we may learn also that we can admire what is greater than ourselves, without thereby personally caring for it as much as for something nearer fitted to us. There is nothing to be ashamed of in such a choice. And if we see the result of meanness, of vanity, of envy, of all the hard sides of man, in his consideration of works of art, so we must beware of the loss of our mental dignity in yielding to our weaker and more amiable side; the caring only for some personal liking, and our coming in that way to what is injustice.

Therein again, personal memories of likings,

memories that fit our inmost nature, would be
allowed to take precedence of those records of
memory which establish greater choices; which
we feel obscurely belong to characters more
highly strung than ours — to beings breathing in
a higher air, more difficult to live in — rarer.

But why should we not be as well pleased to
recognize the fact; why object to what is great
and splendid and lofty and immortal, because we
cannot use it in our every-day life of common,
though happy, moments? Does it hurt me that
Michael Angelo was greater and is greater, while
Carpaccio and Cima are sweet to me, and my
mind makes no effort to comprehend them, but
is simply soothed, as by simple melodies?

Nor is the limit what we can do ourselves,
how far we can leap. Have we not, perhaps,
limited ourselves; and if not, can we alter the
fact by taking thought?

We must not be bound by what we can do, or
what is most akin to what we can do. And
even from what is furthest away from us in art,
we may some day draw the feeling for something

to add to our powers. Or we may see in methods
that are not just our own some fault that helps
us to an expression of an almost contrary feeling.
Much, for instance, of Delacroix's power of expressing melancholy and romantic feeling comes
from his having admired, even against his will,
what may be called the robustious healthiness of
Rubens, and from having actually studied out the
Fleming's material means, which seem usually
so joyous and so unfitted for the Byronic, new
anxieties of this century, distracted by the loss
of old faiths, disturbed by the apparition of new
necessities of inquiry.

"Ses couleurs crues, ses grosses formes,"—Rubens' unbroken colours, his coarse forms, annoyed
Delacroix, but with them he felt the wisdom of
the Fleming and his determination to use any
means for an end. "Cet homme ne se refuse
rien," Delacroix says.

And the great example of Rubens conveyed to
him the idea of a real unity, the presence of a
great life which should animate and sustain both
faults and qualities.

For remember again (as we saw last week) that the wish and the decision to be interested especially in the life and movement of nature, implies another point of view, as well as another method of treatment, from that which would represent pleasure in the quiet, the steadiness and the peace of external sights. From each view and interest a different manner must result.

A man giving even what all expect, sometimes goes very far beyond, and his own record of memories will only be understood as other people's memories accumulate. He will be a constant reminder of there being something more. Little by little, other recorders will make notes that will sustain and justify his; his necessary deficiencies, his necessary exaggerations, will no longer surprise. We shall pass over his bridge to a new land, and thank him whom we doubted at first. It may take a long time; other roads may have been travelled meanwhile, by other explorers whom we notice and whose memories we enjoy; so that Donatello may come fresh to us after several centuries. The Rembrandts, which we recognize as so mighty to-day, whose possession represents so much money, were to be had, even when his name and fame was known, for less than you, my pupils, would accept to-day for any study of yours.

Millet required some twenty years or more to be fairly sure of the Salon; while you, young ladies and gentlemen, if you go to Julien's Academy in Paris for a little while, and are fairly polite, are pretty sure of being accepted where Delacroix was rejected. Perhaps, then, if you have to wait awhile for a real recognition, you will be patient. If it comes later, in a few more years, you can be humble when you think of such names as those I have mentioned.

By asking you to join me in the calm consider- ation of the causes that lead to misapprehension of what the artist has meant — of what he has really said — and of his slow acceptance by us, the world, I have invited you — you who are students with me (though I am named the leader) — to look down in peace upon the battle of the world of art, in which, at another moment, some of us will be combatants.

As in all contemplation, you are placed above the field of strife.

Do not think that you cannot hold, for a moment at least, such a place — that you have of your profession a less high view and less respect. In any museum, worthy of the name in the least, you cannot feel so.

It is your ancestral palace; of whose great inhabitants you are to become worthy. The greatest of reputations belong to your family, — the family ready to adopt you. You too may become heads of great homes, and chiefs of clans, as your kinsmen have been. At least, in some branch you will establish your claim to continue the race — to continue their pursuit; to make also a representation of the world by yourselves.

If there be a place which is yours, it is this, in which there is no lower position except by gradation of service; where rivalry means something more than opposition and triumph over others. For as one of us once said (my old companion in art, Elihu Vedder): "It is not with others we are struggling, as the public think, — it is with ourselves."

And Thackeray, who was with us for a time, as a soldier, and who left us for triumphs in another art, says: "The humblest volunteer in the ranks of art, who has served a campaign or two ever so ingloriously, has at least this good fortune of understanding, or fancying he is able to understand, how the battle has been fought, and how the engaged general won it."

LECTURE V

MAIA, OR ILLUSIONS

SYNOPSIS OF LECTURE V.

The museum a modern make-shift. — Older methods of teaching art.— The Museum and the Academy. — The lesser arts. — The work of art that we call decoration. — Its insufficiency to-day. — Its fulness formerly. — Colour and composition. — Consideration of how we see through the impression of colour. — What we see is translated to us by some effect of coloured light, and that effect is placed within laws of arrangement which sometimes we call perspective and sometimes composition. — Painting and the painter of to-day. — References to the difficulties through which we see. — The illusions and inaccuracies of our senses. — Partial review of artistic vision. — The sight of the moment a theme upon which we embroider former memories, habits and images. — The illusions which we recognize, which prevent our giving to ourselves an accurate account of certain qualities of the things that we look at, can be used in turn in the illusion of the work of art. — The impression of sight connected with the impression of the hand. Hence the touch can designate the mind of the painter. — Time in execution of the work of art not a measurable quantity. — The execution of the work of art implies the joining together of former memories to the perceptions of the moment. Hence the necessity of constant purification of our memories. Hence the use not only of our own, but of the memories of others.

LECTURE V.

MAIA, OR ILLUSIONS.

THE museum, then, is the storehouse which holds the records of your ancestors. It would be better if in the monument of family history only the memories were kept of those who have done honour to our long struggle; and that we should not have any reminder of those who have disgraced us. For them the empty space should be enough, —like the place held in the walls of Venice for the record of Marino Faliero, *Decapitatus pro Criminibus*. But the further that we go back, the more our streams of descent seem clear. Time, as I showed to you before, having disposed of many questions, it is only with the more recent examples that we can become confused. The analogy to all records of ancestry is therefore quite complete. The museum, as you know, is a modern institution. It is admirable in one sense; in another, what it replaces was better for the life of art than what it gives to-day. If it were not so, this age of museums, of collections of general interest in art, of written teaching, of oral explanations, of academies, of government and municipal schools, should have given us the largest and richest development of art which the world has ever seen.

However much the present century has seen done, either in the logical development of art, by the development of the things implied in the memories of older artists, or by the triumphant record of certain men, who here and there, usually in an unforeseen manner, have come to bloom, and have added their stock of memories and their impressions to what we had before — no one, I believe, will consider the statement at all out of the commonplace, that the past centuries, without museums and without academic organization like ours, have given us, not only together, but often separately, proofs of stronger life, of greater technical realization in our arts.

The change was inevitable, and in certain ways we shall have to accept it for an indefinite future. With time we shall readjust ourselves; we shall develop better the methods imposed upon us; it may be that we shall make still stronger what remains we have of the methods of instruction that belong to the past.

Even the destruction now forced by what is called commerce, upon all those branches of art, which, being worked collectively, by many people together of different grades, are specially liable to disturbance which no individual devotion, no individual high-mindedness can check; which also being mechanism, can be made into organizations entirely ruled by the commercial spirit — even these injuries, these degradations, may have an end, when again it may become the interest of what is called commerce to thrive by the rivalry of doing well.

No doubt that with each year the guardians of such vast intellectual property as we detain in museums will feel more and more the responsibility entrusted to them, and will aid by many means the diffusion of their knowledge, the appreciation of the manner of their production; and as the position becomes more and more a function of high educational service, men of learning, men of inquiry, will more and more be chosen to make, by their aiding efforts, common intellectual property of this accumulation.

The breaking up of the old world destroyed the ancient system in which the student of art entered by the gate of the workman — "played in the gate of the Master," as the Japanese called study. He was a child and treated as a child, and things were done for him or not, as might be good for him in the opinion of his betters. Meanwhile he served them. He learned to become a tool, — first the tool of his master and then his own. All instruction went directly with practice, — I do not mean the mere practice of using the hand as we artists use it, but the immediate use of that skill acquired, — for work which had its place already assigned. No detail, therefore, was slurred; and in an art so humble on the side of its execution, so dependent upon materials, there was an unbroken chain between the greatest painter and the man who ground his colours. I think it is again Francis of Holland who speaks of having met Michael Angelo out on his walk, with his old friend and colour-grinder, — a man to whose memory he wrote lines as full of devotion as the great sonnets inspired by what we call his love for Vittoria Colonna. Those relations still subsist in certain countries, as they do in Japan; and this making one family of the greater artist and all who have to do with him has given that peculiar completeness, that sense of peace and absence of struggle which we feel in Japanese art, from the painting of the drawings to the workmanship of their lacquers and their medals.

In those smaller divisions of work in art, which I referred to when I spoke of work done in community, we shall probably see for us some return of the past. But the day of such a natural manner of life may be far off. For our art of painting, the nearest approach to it to-day is still in the schools; but the hold there is a precarious one, and the connection between the greater and smaller is interrupted and dependent upon something else than the necessary progress from first knowledge to full development.

In the older days the master might show his pupils what had been done before them by others than himself, in separate examples, with each of which would go a form of teaching all the more influential from its not being academic. The impression on the younger painter's mind of the great works hung in churches, seen one by one, their colours, their forms distinctly fitted to the place for which they were meant, their meaning emphasized by the circumstances of the place, by the importance attached to the use for which these works of art were meant, must have been far stronger, from its unity, its singleness, than that which students can get to-day from these very same works, confused upon the walls of a building like a museum, not built to hold them more than others; where light falls with democratic indifference, lighting each one impartially, and none of them as they were meant to be lit.

With this division, then, established in the methods of record, the Academy teaching certain things and the Museum all things; the one analytical and in sequence, the other as life teaches, — in a mass of facts, — we come to feel that to bring back the ancient synthesis, the two divisions forced upon us by modern changes must be brought together.

What we need to think of to-day, and in a certain way I am here to show you, is that the Museum knows more than the Academy. In the smaller arts, in that innumerable mass of materials made for use, or what we call mere ornament, — the glass, metal work, carvings of wood and stone, fragments of buildings, leather, tapestry, — the teaching is evident. Every rule has been applied, both those you know and those you have not heard of. It might almost seem at first, if the museum is great enough, that whatever rule has been set down for you will find a contradiction — and a triumphant contradiction — in some small treasure, some choice fragment stored in the collections. In such a case, it will always

be that your teaching has been too narrow, —
probably not narrow so far as any execution may
have gone ; because that of itself carries its own
reasoning, through the use, and sometimes the
predominance, of material; but it will have been
because some question of practice, quite valid, —
even very splendid, — has been put before you
as a principle.

And in no division of the arts of sight has there
been more misapplied ingenuity of teaching, more
narrowness of reasoning, more individual assertion, more professional incapacity, than in the
law-making which has been done in our century,
for the reasonable production of the work of art
that we call decoration. Perhaps there, more
than in our art of painting, is this natural;
because of the less powerful, human, individual
factor and the necessity for the artist of carrying
out such forms of art in conjunction with others,
his superiors in the social management. For he,
individually, does not count so much : his material
is more important than in any other form of art,
— I mean more rebellious, less a creation of his

own (compare at the two extremes a drawing in ink and a stained-glass window); and he works already to supply some wish of others; and he is directed, therefore, somewhat by the taste of the day; somewhat by the larger interests, for instance, of architects, some of whose work he supplies. But whenever one wishes to breathe freely again; whenever one wishes to see freedom in the use of material; whenever one wishes to see the man and not the workshop, the artist and not the trader, the poet, not the schoolmaster, then, tired and disgusted with the present incapacity, — the present deplored, undoubted incapacity, — one shall find in the museums a rest to the mind, and perhaps, as man after all is the same, a hope for the future.

Remember how human the so-called older pieces of little art seem to you, when compared with the modern. Recognize, then, how you come across the result of that same principle which we first recognized, that the man is almost everything, and that anything which does not allow us to feel this is *at once* the imitation and not the reality; be it a piece of machine-made lace,

or a regulation stained-glass window, or the nine-
teenth century carving of a Renaissance façade,
or the fine and silly tooling of a piece of modern
silver.

And do not think that even in the slightest
way, by drawing your attention to what are
called the minor arts, I go outside of what I
am teaching you. If I should ask you to come
upstairs with me, and look at some little piece
of Japanese lacquer, for instance, with a surface
suggesting the weight, as well as the mystery, of
moonlight; with depths of shadow that are typ-
ical of the art of varnish glazes; with irides-
cences like those of living birds or insects; with
sparklings recalling the track of the stars in
water; with patterns firm like the pattern of
a flower; — and all so dwelling in unity that
you cannot think of their being displaced from
the little world of box or tray in which they
live, — so that to the eye, they give the pleasure of notes of music in accord; — if I took you
to look at such a thing, as a lesson, it would be,
among other things, a lesson of what we divide

as colour and composition. That is, as you know, the special line in which the Museum has requested me to direct my teaching. And there is but one way of considering such a division: and that is, that it is almost so large as to include *all* that your eye can possibly light on. You know that what you see is translated to you by some effect of coloured light, and you know that that effect is placed within certain laws of arrangement which we study out in some cases, and call perspective; but which, in other cases, are so obscure, or rather so complicated, that all we can do is to assume that they all must fall within a universal geometry. So that we can feel at ease in the spaces occupied by all the arts that appeal to the sight, and get from each or any what setting right we require.

Perhaps in the way that you think of your drawings, in the way that you make your first drawings in black and white; first, perhaps, from casts, then from the model placed in a light before you, which allows you to see it more by light and shade than by its local colour,

— that is to say, by that flesh-colour which it
has in common with all other flesh, — you have
learned to think of your impression of sight as
having been first a sight of black and white,
or a sight of form.

Let us remember our consideration of how, on
the contrary, this representation by what we
call a drawing, of light and colour and shadow
(determined by an edge) was recognized by us
as being, on the contrary, a final synthesis — a
sort of abstraction; that you or the savage began at the final end, which was a brief and
violent summing up of all seen, in the least real
of all possible expressions. You will remember
that the savage, by two long lines, which he
swept from an imaginary central one and in
opposition, gave you a shape of a fish, that is
to say, with two black lines which did not
exist (for there are no black lines that constitute a fish; there are only the edges of the
place which the fish occupies and a résumé of
thousands of these edges in one); that these two
or three lines represented a surface brilliant

and shining in colour; covered with hard scales, flecked with dots and patches; glistening with muscular action; itself placed, if in the water, against a moving luminous background and involved in it; or if thrown, let us say, upon the grass, against a background formed of multitudes of dots and lines of light and shadow, and patches of transparency, of a colour as uniform, as soft and rich as the surface of the fish was many-coloured and iridescent. Can anything be more abstract, as I showed you, than the fact that these two things that do not exist give you the image of the fish?—provided always that you have seen a fish. Had you never seen one, or anything like it, that fish would not exist in this drawing. Suppose, on the contrary, that we could paint in some approximate way after nature; and give the colours, the brilliancy, the light and shade which make the appearance of the creature and determine its form — determine the way that we think it would feel if we put our hand on it — and that behind that fish we could render adequately the surface or surfaces of the grass. Then, though you might not have seen one, you would be incalculably nearer the certainty of the reality of the meaning of these marks. Roughly, I might say, you would see the fish and recognize some sort of animal unknown to you.

You have probably been well taught — I may say certainly; but many of us have not been better taught; and we are often made to believe that the first objects that our memory of sight recalls — and hence reproduces — are not colours and light, but really form. And we are told so because with most men colour does not seem to be the thing of most interest. That may be perfectly true — it may be perfectly true of the artist, even of the artist of highly organized temperament and of great culture; but the two questions should not be confused. Our sensation is one thing and the conscious interest that we take in the sensation is another; as it is we who do the thing, our record being a record of our interest in the matter, if we delight in this or in that, and we make a record of it so far as we are artists, we can be satisfied; as it might be if, instead of taking an interest in the representation of the thing, we took an interest in its classification, as scientific men might do, — nay, even in its profit to us by sale or purchase, as merchants might do. But its sensation to us, which we translate into what we wish, is a luminous coloured sensation.

Of course I refer to the eye which is sensitive in what we call the normal way — that is to say, is not colour-blind. Whether the eye of man was originally so, or has gradually become so, and the deadness to colour impressions of a part of the retina is a remnant of an earlier, less cultured stage, is out of my line, and practically has very little value; like the question, whether the savage, or the ancient Greek, who was perfect in all things but that, would have less perception of colour because he did not carry the whole dictionary in his mind.

The fact that the colour has no name to the person who recognizes it, is of no consequence to us painters. We all know that we painters find it extremely difficult to tell the names of colours to outsiders, while we can reproduce them in a way that they cannot. So with the savage whom I have met, and whose vocabulary is so slight that red and purple and orange have a similar name, the slightest change of colour in fruit or leaves, or the plumage of animals, or the scales of fish, or the surface of the sea, or the moisture of the atmosphere, is detected, in a way to make even a careful painter ashamed of his miserable colour training.

As the savage, after all, uses his observation of these colours for another purpose than the enjoyment of the colours themselves, to him they are indications rather of the form or of the state of the thing; and possibly, if I were to examine him, he would rather give me an account of it in such a way as to eliminate the colour and describe the form. We only fix our attention upon our sensations insomuch as we can use them for the knowledge of exterior objects. Hence, for a good many of us, notwithstanding that we recognize certain things only by the variation of colour, we only think of them as in their usefulness to us. If, for example, the fruit that a boy took up were deficient in colour, and in that way showed him that it is not ripe — he would eat it all the same, I know, but he would know very well what it was that he was eating; and we who are no longer boys would reject it.

If, for example, I meet a friend whose colour strikes me as altered, who is pale, yellowish, whose lips are no longer red, whose hair seems less rich, what I say and what I think is, "He is ill." The sensation of colour that I have received is translated into an intellectual description; but this very fact, we will see, proves that I have stored away a whole treasure-house of colour impressions, since I compare them again with the colour impression of the moment.

The illustrations that I could give would be so numerous, that I shall only call up that one which occurs to me from having looked, a moment ago, at the surface of some china, which surface, by its colour and light, by the exact value, as we painters call it, — the amount of brilliancy, — and suggestion of material by that exact brilliancy, — decided for me the question of its authenticity.

The question of the pleasure that we take in recalling this freshness of the first impressions, all made through light and colour, is the question of the pleasure one takes in painting; that is to say, in abstaining from abstraction, and trying to give a full result in keeping with the wish of recording the face of the world, in such a way that the actual voice of nature, in its first call to us, is still fresh in our memory.

Examples might help you : might mitigate the harshness of such general statements as the pressure of time obliges me to make. Were I carrying out these readings (as they well might be carried out) into long talks, where the hazards of the moment would allow me to modify the use of examples, by cautioning you in regard to what part of my examples I wished you to see, I should state nothing without some reference to a thing of present sight. But no museum would be large enough for one side, and on another I should need the scientist's apparatus to make you follow delicate experiments.

I say this because it occurred to me, but a moment ago, that I might use some painting from above, in the Museum, to draw your attention to the fulness of my meaning when I speak of painting and of the painter — in the strictest sense, the more modern one — and speak of what painting gives in its greatest power of mirroring the world.

We are speaking as if we were judges, and as I said to you, we are speaking of some one of our family, when we discuss any artist and appreciate him as if we were his equals. Let us take some painting by Mr. Bonnat. If you will remember how we described the methods of the engraver, his patchwork and crossed lines, you can put yourself perfectly in the place of the artist accustomed to such illusions of sight in black and white, who will see nothing but what his eye is accustomed to when he notices that Mr. Bonnat models fingers and hands and flesh, with strokes and markings of black like those of the engraver.

As I told you, for him they melted in his eye at once; while another artist, less accustomed to reduce things seen to black and white equations, would see these tones more separately, as if they had been transferred to a painting from an engraving. You might tell me that you saw things so, if you explained to me while you were copying the method of Mr. Bonnat.

As far as you can see anything, you might perhaps go so far as to tell me that you saw things modelled in that direction; that is to say, that these curves represented curves which described the sense of modelling. They are half-way between the intention of a painter and a sculptor.

Admire Mr. Bonnat for his success in using this other method, without injuring the meaning of his work; but when you think of what you see, remember better, as a record of absolute observation, the splendid portraits of Rembrandt which Mr. Havemeyer once loaned to the Museum. There, naively, like a child, like a great man, like a Shakespeare in prose, Rembrandt filled in

every space, as if he had never known any method
of any other art. Flesh tone followed flesh tone,
and tints of clothing and of hair, of fur, of linen,
followed each other in a mosaic of adjustment
so perfect as to make the French painter look
like an engraver in colourless material. Of course
there is injustice in the actual words that I use;
between the two men there is no comparison as
painters, but there is as seekers after character,
as placers of the individual human being before
you. Hence Mr. Bonnat loses nothing by the
photograph; sometimes even he is better there;
or in the engraving, the birthplace of certain
parts of his manner of painting.

The functioning of our perceptions of sensations
of the very simplest character is so automatic
that it is not often possible to make their existence
evident to every one. In a general way, as we
all know, we conceive with most trouble that
thing the possession of which is to us the most
familiar and the most certain. The actions of
our organization are so much ourselves that we
certainly never realize in action their enormous

complication and their possible subdivision by analysis.

From the point of view of a painter, then, the painter as I at first defined him, — the painter of our day, the artist anxious to analyze in the construction of his work, as he synthesizes in the effect of it upon us, — what we see first is not form, but lights, colours, colours that contrast, and colours that are broken or mixed. The sensation of coloured space or extent leads for the painter to that of a solid image, and his work of art is what has been called an equation of light.

However abridged and transposed is our representation, we are urged to it through a desire to enter into the intimacy of nature; and in establishing that relation, we have to bring in the use of faculties which we divide, when we try to classify them, into faculties of perception, attention and memory. Our organism records impressions after the original excitement of them has passed. Consecutive images persist for a time, and through this persistence of culture by us our faculty becomes stronger. Even in what we suppose to be inattention, — in what we call absent-mindedness, — memories are readjusted which we recall afterwards, and we say, "I remember now that there was such and such a thing." Or even we may say, "There was just something I don't remember."

We readjust, perhaps with greater difficulty, things that we owe to our visual memory. If it were possible to compare music with painting, we should feel convinced that it is easier to recall the details of a piece of music than of a painted composition. Any one can notice — even ourselves, the painters — how much sooner we can remember a melody than we can recall with similar certainty the arrangement of a painting. With each of us, also, the intensity of what might be called our sight, that is to say, the strength of the momentary impression and the recrudescence of the same later, through memory, varies extremely. With certain eyes the colour space, with others the edge of that space, — the outline, — remains more distinctly. With us, the use of the hand, which translates into muscular energy the attention given by the eye, is the form which records our memories, and which to a great extent recalls them to us — forces them back, through some extraordinary connection. The hand would then have a special memory, and later I shall draw your attention to it.

You will remember how we clearly saw that drawing from life is an exercise of memory. It might be said that the sight of the moment is merely a theme upon which we embroider the memories of former likings, former aspirations, former habits, images that we have cared for, and through which we indicate to others our training, our race, the entire educated part of our nature. It is so much so that this memory of the more conventional side of our artistic feeling is organized more easily than that of the colour and light, — that is to say, the real momentary impression that we receive.

For hundreds of artists who have done great things in the record of their teaching and their love of abstractions of line, for instance, there

is not more than one who has recorded for us
the magic of colour, the mystery of light. In
other words, the man of line is far less rare than
the man of light.

Could we devote some special time to it, we
might consider how we are so accustomed to
see with our two eyes that it is difficult for
us to get a representation of what the single
eye would do. In the rapid review of the technique, if I may so call it, of artistic vision, we
shall be obliged to put aside any present consideration of this question of the manner in
which we make out of these different sights a
single sight; and how, in reality, with them
both, we never see simply. But you can recall
how the single circle of each side of the opera-
glass melts into an oval; how we see with one
eye to a greater depth; how with two we
broaden our sight; how with the habit of seeing
surfaces larger with two eyes than with one, we
exaggerate the size of smaller objects; how we
disfigure with the two eyes a small square, for

instance, which seems to us higher than it is wide, as long as we fix it, while it becomes wider as we see it from the side. It would certainly be of use to us to go through the question in a lengthy way, because, though the artist has worked from the beginning without help of such analysis, still all reasoning about his use of this first necessary tool, the eye, will give him the advantage of a sort of gymnastics, a sort of hygienic exercise, which may occasionally help him in moments of doubt, or may, on the other hand, reconcile him with those difficulties which arise from his constitution, and which he might otherwise ascribe to the objects outside of him, whose adequate memorial he desires to preserve. Or else he might imagine that he had more special difficulties peculiar to himself, and lose that directness which is one of his greatest charms. But he might be relieved, for instance, from being troubled too much at finding that one eye sees colour in a different way from the other, and asking himself which one is right. Or, as you were probably taught at first, he will know that the photograph, which is of such use to him, which helps him out of so many difficulties, by preserving memories of sight that he cannot remember, by its cold-blooded indifference, by its sudden perception of fleeting accidents — that the photograph gives him only an image seen by one eye.

And as to the very capacity of sensation, we know how much that varies with each personal factor, — with age, with our habit of noticing, with the way we feel at the time, and with our practice. He who has learnt to work in a faint light ends by seeing as clearly as he who works in much light; although the outside light be not the same for each. And, conversely, you may have noticed that the landscape before you, which at first is so radiant with light as to contrast strongly in your mind with the tone of the objects seen within doors, assumes, after a time, greater depth of colour, a greater amount of modelling, consequently a greater proportion of shadow. So much so, that working a whole day in the sunshine enables one to consider the depth of colour-

ing as of equal interest with the brightness and
intensity of light which was the first impression.[1]

Need I speak of the illusions produced by the
contrast of a colour? Need I go into the difficulty of adjusting that relation between the oppositions of colour and our eye, — those it detects in
nature, and the necessity that we have to reproduce these analogies, to reinforce them or to
weaken them, because the luminous scale of
nature is not enclosed within the limit of our palette, and light has to be translated into pigment?
These complementary analogies are felt by us
where they are perhaps only indicated or supposed
to exist in nature.[2]   Here what I should like to

---

[1] You will remark that this fact widens enormously the range of
the "plein air," "out of doors," rendering between extremes of
depth and lightness.

[2] My friend, Mr. Roelke, has pointed out to me the following ex-
tract, which confirms our perceptions of the early instinct of artists as
such.

"The artist could derive little advantage from that theory with
which the optician, with his negative efforts, explained the phenomena
which took place.   For although he and the other spectators admired
the bright colours of the prism and felt their harmony, yet it always
remained an enigma for him, to know how to distribute them among

have would be the knowledge of a lecturer whom you heard last winter, whose name is everywhere associated with the question of colour. With such a great dictionary of information, of experiment, I should be able to touch lightly on the subject, and yet to give you the suggestion of what you have either read about, or will read about when you wish to be thoroughly informed of how we feel colour, and through it see, in a more masculine way, the means of recording it. I refer to Professor Rood of Columbia College, whose writings were a consolation to me long ago, in my

the objects which he had formed and arranged according to certain conditions.

"A great portion of the harmony of a picture depends upon the light and shade; but the proportion of colours to light and shade was not so easily discovered, and yet every painter could soon see that his picture could attain perfection only through the combination of both harmonies, and that it was not sufficient to mix a colour with black or brown to make it the proper colour for shading. Many experiences, in conjunction with an eye favoured by nature, the practice of feeling, delivery, and the example of great masters, brought artists to a high degree of excellence, although they could hardly communicate the rules according to which they acted; by looking at a large picture gallery, one can easily convince oneself of the fact that every master has had a different way of handling colours." — GOETHE, *Contributions to Optics*, 1791, Introduction.

attempts at disentangling what was right in my instinctive apparitions.

And not only must the painter gather together these effects of light, both those he thinks are objective, — that is to say, are discerned by him outside, — and those that are subjective, — that is to say, are translated through him, by his own exaggeration or his own diminution in rendering, — but he must also obtain the effects of relief in the same way, by simplification or exaggeration. On a flat surface he must give the sense of space, and accommodate the two visions, of the one eye, for which he has perspective, and of the two eyes, which cannot be traced by geometry. Representation then, in comparison of the phenomena of light, demands reflection and practice. I believe that Kant has said that " our senses do not deceive because they do not judge. All illusion is to be charged to the intellect, which often misjudges the material offered by the senses." Which otherwise might be transposed into saying that our senses always deceive us, more especially the sense of sight; for there are no luminous rays that are blue or red or so forth ; but certain rays, of different wave-lengths, wake up within us, through some mechanism of our organization, a sensation of what we call blue or red. It is for our intellect to know these illusions and to put them in order, to weaken them or strengthen them, to enforce and illustrate them, to ennoble them through our admiration, and through that love to make them beautiful.

.   .   .   .

Let us think of a few of the appearances of things which misinterpret other facts behind them. The list is endless.

Equally lit, a long-waved colour is more important than a short-waved colour. Frank complementary discontinuities, as, for instance, black and white, bright red and deep green, may emphasize the division of coloured spaces, but render all the more difficult the comparative gauge of their real dimensions. To any one accustomed to draw, in the usual way, a colourless object, it will be difficult to avoid mistakes when translating into

black and white a model of one complementary
colour placed against its complementary background. A long rectangle, tinted in its upper
half by a long-waved colour, in its lower half by
a short-waved colour, will appear larger above
than below. The space comprised between two
light lines upon a dark ground will seem narrower
than the same space enclosed between two dark
lines on a light ground. The distances between
the stars seem to diminish when the moon shines
in the sky near them. Two black lines which
appear parallel traced upon a white ground, no
longer seem so if the end of one be tinted with
light red, and the extremity of the other with
dark blue. Two red flowers on a green ground
seem nearer, one to the other, than two blue
flowers; the light gains in size and the dark loses
in proportion.

These illusions which we recognize, which prevent our giving to ourselves an accurate account
of certain properties, certain qualities of the things
that we look at, we can ourselves use in the illusion that we now in turn shall create in our work

of art. The last examples that I have just given you, if you have had any practice at all, will occur to you as means of increasing the appearance of space or of depth, or of narrowing and diminishing the same, and these means have been used by painters from early times.

And here I remember a deception of sight that I have occasionally referred to with my pupils, when they insisted that they were able to judge absolutely of the size or length of some given space or line. Here are two lines, which you see are of equal length, and at the extremities of each I draw four lines meeting them in opposite ways.

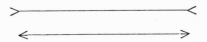

As you see, our first lines have changed their length; and what is strange, when I wipe the first line out, the spaces which both of them traversed still continue to appear different in length, though we know they are not.

This is again a double lesson. You can see the variations that in your work — which is an imitation of the effect of nature — you can produce, without the alteration of what might be called real dimension; whether this be by modelling or by opposing lines. When you cheat in your little world of imitation, you do not cheat any more than the great world about you deceives you. And for a moment yet I will detain you on the edges of this endless field of illusion.

Our sense of certain sensations becomes dulled by habit. In our usual attitude we feel colour and size less intensely; but should we displace the eyes, should we throw our head to one side, the colours become more intense, more driven in, one upon the other; and the heights that we see with the usual vision change with this displacement.[1] Often you have been surprised by what seemed the newer beauty of the landscape, the mountains, the sky, the cloud above, reversed in the mirror of the lake. The whole scene reversed

[1] Very recent experiments testify to a real change in the colour- and form-fields.

is reinforced also, — the gradation of colour, the sense of modelling, the sense of retreat of the upper surfaces of leaves upon leaves, the receding flanks of the mountain, the more evident poise of the cloud in mid-air. And notice that in all your delight, you have thought of it as a painting.

So also we are deceived because we know, and things in the distance retain somewhat the size that we know they have; as in the painting of the early masters the human figure keeps, even in the distance, the proportion of its natural superiority. In faint lights, in the twilight, in the fog, the importance of objects that we desire to see makes them change their apparent size, and deceives us as to what they are.

And we are deceived — but that you do not know as I do — in the spaces and sizes of the landscapes of our childhood. When we see them again, they are measured by another scale. We do not know if all men see with an equal scale; and we cannot even know whether the image that we receive ourselves remains alike from its first apparition to our losing it.

No light is immovable; and it may be said that to reproduce life is to reproduce the fluctuations of the movement of light; whether it be the glance of the eye, the play of the smile on the lips, — that expression so visible, so evasive when fixed by our eye, of intellectual capacity, — or again, the movement of the body in gesture, or the strain of muscles in action.

Still life, as it is called when thought of as art, is still nature animated; for the slight movement of shadows, the glistening waves of air, the shadowing of clouds, are all expressions of movement; and, indeed, is it not because of this that at certain moments, when the change is slow or gradual, we feel as if the surface of nature slept?

We see a number of points of light that are joined, apparently one to another, as making a continuous line, as we see in more exaggerated cases the line of fire described by a torch that is waved, or the straight lines given by the fall of drops of rain. For the eye which *sees*, the bird that flies has more than two wings; he

may have four. The horse at full pace has
more than four legs; he has at least eight. It
is for us to adjust this multiplicity of sights,
and in some way render the appearance of continual fluctuation. Hence, for many painters —
for those who have been especially fond of life,
of animation, for whom action and passion have
been of most importance, or who, like Rubens,
have insisted beyond everything upon the living-
ness of their self-created world — comes a fear of
petrifying the figures that they paint, by too sharp
and rigid renderings, and they try to avoid suggesting that their eye has been able to follow
in quiet all the details which they had before
them.

So also, very often, the intimation of an unfin-
ished sketch, the help given to the illusion in
the suggestion of movement by the keeping of
more outlines than one; by the artist's not effac-
ing slight variations in these outlines, by even
keeping sometimes the general plan indicated
within which the attitudes are expressed.

There is a great deal of truth in a statement

of Véron, in his work on Æsthetics. And many
of you who have seen the drawings that he
mentions can appreciate the meaning of his criticism. "Sketches," he says, "are in general
more living than completed drawings; and some
years ago we saw rather a striking example of
this. *The Gazette des Beaux-Arts* had published
in fac-simile a certain number of sketches of Mr.
Baudry, for his work in the Opera House.
They had an animation and life in great part
lost in the painted work. Gestures, however,
were not wanting in the paintings of Mr. Baudry. One might even say that he had been prod-
igal of them, and yet 'cela ne remue pas,' —
and yet all is stationary. All these personages,
notwithstanding their long arms, their stretched-
out legs, are fixed in an immobility all the more
disagreeable because it contrasts with their supposed movements. Why," he continues, "such
a disastrous transformation? On this account,
because in the sketches these gestures were indicated by a multiplicity of neighbouring outlines,
which, owing to this very neighbourhood, ani-

mated the figures by marking their several movements — that is to say, several successive attitudes,
all perceived within the same movement; while
in the one only and precise outline of the final
rendering, this mixture of succession and of simul-
taneousness has completely disappeared."

Without insisting upon the excellence of his
choice in this case, — for Mr. Baudry was a most
elegant and refined painter, — there is something
fundamentally true in these remarks of the French
critic.

Hence in the very movement of the brush, one
wishes to see the sensation of movement deeply
felt. Hence our annoyance at the crystallization
of movement given to us in the instantaneous
photograph, that makes of a sea of water a sea of
hardened metal.

I have connected, as you will see, the impression of sight with the impression of the hand.
The voluntary attention of the artist is trans-
formed into muscular energy, ending in the repro-
duction of images by the hand, and forms the
first part of an extremely complicated process,

which even this motion of the hand does not fully discharge; for there are still the controlling of possible errors by the sight, exercised again, and by that power of thought which is behind everything. The hand will even act, as it were, as we recognize in drawings that we make without our looking at them, even while we think of other things, — or in the extraordinary way in which, when ordered, the hand will work while we converse with our model. The professional portrait painter in that way carries out most astonishing disassociations, when he draws out, for instance, the political notions of some sitter whom he is anxious to place at his ease, — and seems to us, who are not in the secret of his interior life, more absorbed in conversation than in his painting.

The hand, too, as we said before, has a certain memory of its own, and works, as you will remember, more easily upon accustomed surfaces — even such as are not facile; as the opposing sand I spoke of, in which the young savages traced their images. We have all gone through the suggestiveness of a pleasant paper presented to tools that we felt would suit us. We feel the materials responsive to what they are really going to express ourselves. I told you that the very touch expresses yourself.

It expresses either your being yourself, or your striving to be Mr. So-and-so. It expresses your great anxiety to repeat the movement of light in nature; the manner in which your sense of form has been awakened ; your sense of the depth of things as they receded, of the distinctness or indistinctness with which you see certain parts of the luminous coloured spectacle before you.[1] It shows whether you analyze by separating or by grouping together your impressions ; whether you keep adding fact to fact, as in a catalogue, or whether you choose deliberately, or whether you subordinate, making one point you have detected in your sight more important than others, and letting others derive from it. It will look careful, and merely patient and attentive ; or again, as if

[1] For we must not forget that painting represents not only what we see, but what we do not see.

you were impressed by the endless mystery of
what you see. It will look cock-sure, as if you
didn't find so much in things, after all; or it may
look as if you admired the beautiful swing with
which you did things. And it will surely tell
whether that is *all* you know, or whether you have
a store of memories, only implied and not brought
out.

Hence the touch of a great master is something
not to be rivalled, except with a similar equipment
of memory of the eye, and an equally developed
memory of the hand.

Nor indeed have we attained the mastery of
our execution until the hand can work almost
by itself.

Should you, indeed, attempt to copy the final
work of a Rembrandt or a Velasquez, — which
is final synthesis of all his manners of work,
a method built upon enormous series of memories
preserved or rejected, — should you attempt this,
you will see that you have only been able to copy
a part of the top of the paint, the look of the
surface of the colour; and that even your move-

ment of hand has not — and naturally enough —
the ease that comes of extraordinary practice.
Hence you will never wish to repeat motions
that you cannot well (I shall not say *fully*) understand; as if you repeated the action of the hands
of the conjurer, without being able to accomplish
his ends, — his making you take the card he
wishes, or his being able to draw out of your
pockets things that you know never were there.
But if you repeat his processes of study, with
similar disposition of mind and body, then the
action of his hand will come in normally, and
have all the value of a gesture meaning something.

And in this simplification of the use of the word
touch, do not think I mean only the actual contact
of a fraction of a second. There is no time in
the work of art. The long processes of a Dutch
painter (or a Venetian) are all one thing : the
firm foundation of drawing; the graduated *underneaths*, as painters call them; the veilings of their
washes, or half-opaque coverings of paint; the
glazings ; the retouchings ; the scumblings ; the

draggings of coloured substances, are all *one thing*, just as much as the single drop of india ink put on a *kakemono* by the artist of Japan.

It is only another way of expressing the multitudinousness of nature, by different forms of synthesis; and if you think that the Japanese manner of running a brush full of ink, on paper or silk, is a short way, try it. In their schools they give many years — a length of time which would appall your young Western minds — eight years perhaps — to get an adequate representation of the touch which characterizes the school. And, indeed, it might happen with them that one might hear what I have heard: " So-and-so of a couple of hundred years ago can no more be copied. The last man is dead who had the secret transmitted to him through all this time, and cultivated by him all his life. So that it is not to be hoped that any one will begin it all over again in Japan."

Let us never be deceived by the slight rapidity of a few moments or a few years. In a supposed case, were a painter to devote all his life to one

painting; could he do so; were he great enough
to do so; to make a vase strong and fine enough
to hold these feelings of his whole age, — he would
only have occupied a little piece of time, dispro-
portionate in relation even to the continuous existence in time of the world he attempts to mirror.

In the execution of his work the artist is
brought, even by the mere mechanical progress
of the work, to a recall of all his latent consciousness. In all that we do freely, in our perception
of things, we are obliged to join together, at every
moment, thousands of former visual memories,
recent or very old, to the perceptions of the
moment. From the first movement of the hand
to the last — even, as I said, from the first sight
of the paper or the canvas on which the painter
is to draw, every moment when he thinks of
work, all the accumulated images come back to
him, and have a right upon him. Some he will
welcome, others he must reject; what he has that
is good of his previous education will be source of
strength; where he has made mistakes, where he
has been badly taught, where he has been incom-

petent or inattentive, he will suffer later, in these very memories. In a certain way, what he is really entering upon is a discovery of himself in an order fatally marked for him. The block of marble of which Michael Angelo speaks, which contained all that the greatest artist could ever find, is himself. In the long run he may be sure that he will discover himself; and the slow-grown genius is often not the least great. Hence the necessity of constant work; hence the necessity of constant purification of our memories; hence the use, not only of our own memories, but of the memories of others, such as are gathered about us. What we can feel sure of is that nothing has been done once for all — that all the illusions, the realities, have not yet been reproduced through other illusions, and that no matter how completely all has been done, all the more chance for you to do it again: to make once for all, another time, the Runner, the Sower, the Thrower of the Disc; to paint again, as for the last time, the great sea and rushing waterfall. That one window open upon the world through each great artist is closed for you, but out of all others you can look, and within their frame make your own picture of the world again. The very fact that it has all been done is enough to assure you that it can be done again, as never before.

LECTURE VI

SINCERITY

SYNOPSIS OF LECTURE VI.

The contemplation of nature has moved the mind of man to expression. — Its contradictions make us realize in art an order made by us according to our reason. — In the work of art man is the measure of all things. — Meaning of the word *design*. — Confusion in the work of art of methods belonging to different memorial systems. — This confusion a blot in the logical balanced world of art, usually brought about by appropriation of the works of others. — Self-righteousness and belief in made-up formulas. — Dependence upon a grammar meant for other purposes.—The formulation of practice as principle.—Consequent dishonesty. — Every complete record of sight must contain a record of our ignorance. — The attitude of the child. — It is absurd to copy the memories of others so as to pass them off as our own : it is profitable to copy them so as to purify our own. — Donatello, Niccolo Pisano, Raphael, Michael Angelo, Rubens. — As our art is composed of visual memories, or affected by them, so memories of thought outside of what affects handiwork will either elevate or degrade art. — The subject is merely the place where we express ourselves. — The sculptor Socrates, the painters Euripides and Pyrrho. — There is no art without a craft. — Value of all methods that can avail. — Good language is learned by living among people who can themselves speak well.

LECTURE VI.

SINCERITY.

If before now I have sufficiently brought to
your minds the quality of the memories upon
which we build; if we keep in mind how we work
with prejudices of sight, or how often we entangle one matter of seeing or recording sight
with another, it may seem that though we are
always on the threshold, on the edge of originality, — that is to say of a personal solution of all
memories in a unity, — we can each have a very
little of it, to leaven the mass with; but yet that
a very little of personal power will represent a
great factor.

In that way I could say again that all is to do
over again; and again that if it happened to
you to have the extreme honour of re-inventing,
you will have the delight of having made in

your own self the experiment of ages. Over that bridge the least variation will bring you into newer worlds.

Always has man been interested in nature in a contemplative manner. I mean by nature what is outside of ourselves, man included, his meaning, his constitution, as well as the world he inhabits, its laws and its appearances. The enchantments of nature and her disillusions; the caresses and cares she has for us, her supreme indifference to our individual existence, have in turn moved the mind of man to expression. The struggles of moral good against the evil that reigns in the world; the battle of will against blind fate; the presence of the constant pain and sorrow which are the basis of life; the law of death for which everything lives, — have in turn been spectacles to warm or chill.

On this basis have rested the foundations of love and pity, of courage, of law, and of all the virtues.

The contradictions of the world of existence; its over-profusion; its escaping at every point from any fixed comprehension; its suggesting the opposite; its constantly taking in our eyes the appearance of a world of chance, — makes us realize in art another world, which has some rules, some order made to our size, to our reason.

In the made-up stories of art all is explained. They come to an end deliberately chosen; every detail is used for some purpose of that very story; and when we close the binding of the book, we really come to an end.

It is not so in nature: but in art the end, the meaning, is for us; we are the final cause; in the work of art "man is the measure of all things." Each form of art is a restoration of nature to what she should be; an emphasis of some hidden view that escapes us, otherwise, from the size of the entire world. So that we recognize, with the relief that we call the sense of art, in the forms of architecture, the setting forth of a geometry, — a proportion which the tangled world contains, it is true, but does not set out clear and unmixed, without contradictions, without hesitation and weakening. The faint curves are made into geometric ones; the horizontal and the perpendicular, which are abstractions, become now concrete — one might say living; everywhere all is developed in an order implied within the idea of structure. Gradually there is no form in nature which does not supply some suggestion of abstract form, and is not told of in some settled form whose final establishment is a creation of man.

And so in the arts that connect with architecture; which are mistakenly said to be derived from it, — I say mistakenly, because the instinct of order, of repetition, of balance, of assertion and discovery of geometric form, is as evident in the pearl-bead bracelet of a savage girl, invented and used long before buildings were built, as in any form of what we call decoration.

But we delight in finding some such arrangement in the face of nature herself; we choose our place for looking at her features; we place ourselves so as to emphasize some of these abstract properties of things; we so place ourselves

that we can most feel certain curves, certain per-
pendiculars, certain horizontals, certain arrangements of triangular spaces. For a rough example,
in looking at a waterfall, we may choose some
place whence we can feel the under curve and
the masses of the upper water, their curves and
breaking, and the return curves of the splashing
water. We may take into our sight a tall cliff
or a tree on one side; so as to have the illusion
of depth or height increased. And so for any
other choice. Our *way of looking* at things is
composition. So that it might be said that we
compose in our very way of looking at nature,
without ever thinking of any copy, any imitation of this appearance of nature in art. And
we say that this or that is more beautiful, meaning that beauty is the thing that we love, as it
takes form for us, through our choice.

The following of this detection of a plan, which
in its extreme shape, a sort of grammatical analysis, gives us the Moorish geometric decoration,
leads us to seek also for what we call the line;
meaning the ornamental line which we think we

discover, and which we discover for the purpose
of bringing what we see a little closer to a design; that is to say, in the original meaning of
the word *design*, an intention, a purpose, a human arrangement of the present for the future.
The more strongly we feel this, the more important the result of our work; because all the
more does it insist upon that primal intention
of reducing nature to art. That is to say, of
insisting upon the law and order implied, — a
law not always apparent in a world full of accidents which we cannot reduce to order.

Compare the fateful look of one of Millet's
figures, with the accidental, haphazard appearance of a figure of what might be the same
peasant doing the same thing, in the work of
smaller artists — if indeed it be quite fair to compare them, because not seldom the weakness of
observation runs through every detail of the painting of the smaller man.

Not seldom the peasant himself, the subject of
the picture, does not make his traditional gestures
in a full and complete manner: as also, not sel-

dom, does the animal (who is, however, yet nearer
to the law of nature) step poorly, stand poorly,
make a deficient equation. The reign of accident,
of contradiction, runs into and interferes with the
government of law which we are looking for.
Notice how in the reflection of the world of sound
by the art of music, the musician does not seek
to represent its possible violations, its breaks of
harmony.

So that Millet turned one day to a friend and
said, "Do you do this motion for me. The peas-
ants here cannot carry it out as it should be.
The lines they make do not fill anything."
Whenever I look upon the engraving of the drawing which he then made, I have the satisfaction of
a standing lesson upon what composition means.

The hand of which we have spoken as having
a memory of its own, follows these lines of our
choice, until at length, almost of its own accord,
it traces curves, and divides spaces which recall
the order that we call ornament. All of you
know this more or less, and you also know that
even when your mind knows, the hand will not

always obey. We have been speaking of composition, and you see that the detection of its existence in our impressions of nature accompanies more or less all full artistic sight. Roughly we can determine some of the preferences of its laws. The whole world of ornamental art is based upon them. In our more plastic arts the geometric law is more difficult to disentangle; because our arts include the representation of that part of exterior nature where accident has its place more distinctly; where the energies of animal life may be part of the picture; where moral and intellectual life may be implied. For remember that for us, just now, nature is all that is outside of our innermost, unanalyzed self, and that the moral life expressed in living beings is nature for us just as truly as plant life or crystallization of minerals.

You will have remembered and kept steadily in mind our considerations when we have paused for a time in the discussion of memories of education, of training, of rule given to us from without, and their entanglement with the memories collected by ourselves, either in the remote or the imme-

diate past. We have also dwelt upon the confusion in the work of art of methods of interpretation
belonging to different memorial systems. Such
confusions are extremely frequent; they can be
lived through, it is true, by a strong personality,
by one who feels the fundamental rule, namely,
that all methods are man's property, that methods
are for art, not art for methods; yet his needs are
not necessarily yours, and if you have the least
choice you cannot employ his without bringing
out more fully in your work this irrational, contradictory side which may be all right in the world
of chance, but not in the logical, balanced world
of art. Strange to say, some of the greatest blun-
ders, some of the most annoying sufferings of
sight, have been brought about by this error, this
want of comprehension, have come in just where
their authors were encouraged to feel that they
had been obeying the law, — nay, were proud and
self-righteous about their obedience, or rather their
testimony, and considered that knowing that they
had the true faith, they had but to keep to the
rule and shut their eyes.

But though in this they were not different from many of other schools, who also think that the conscience of their own eyes need no longer be considered, — they and all are in risk who forget that in art there is no collective salvation. Its theology is as cruel as that mediæval view of the future which made Dante place popes and priests in the singing flames of the Inferno.

And each man is judged by himself.

You will remember that I referred, in a previous lecture, to the evidences in the work of certain painters which prove that they retain a memory of colourless representations — or perhaps I ought to say of black and white representations — of nature, within their other memories of the dress that nature always assumes, which is a coloured one. We called up our recollections of paintings which looked as if studied from plaster casts or statues, and of paintings that represent movement fixed and frigid as the cast; of paintings wherein are preserved methods of black and white memories; of engraving, of drawing with pencil or with crayon; of paint-

ings where the entire surface, even the movement of the brush, transfers to your eye the
sensation, not of a vacillating coloured atmosphere, but of the steady, measurable world that
lives in engravings. We made out the causes
to have been the persisting memories of things
already made within the immediate memories of
things seen. It was useless to go further and
to imply that the colourless representation is an
easier and more measurable — more commercial
— manner of carrying out the form, the appearance of a painting, so as to make it understood
by many or most — therefore more negotiable.
We might also notice that, connected with this
obsession in the way of having the colourless
representation, already made, direct for us what
is apparently our fresh perception, we may also
suffer from an obsession of arrangements — of
composition as it is called, by which we single
out certain arrangements, certain divisions, that
we have already seen made artificially, and seek
to impose them upon the face of nature, — either
that nature which we see at the moment, or

the nature which we see in our minds, and which is the memory of outside perceptions. For example, there was a time when the very landscape painter, apparently, forced the arrangement of what he saw into a set mould already provided. Or else — and it has lingered to our day — he arranged what we call his imagined pictures into some similarly conventional division of light and shade, for instance, or of distribution of masses.

Nor can we think that we can escape from such a fate merely because, in the studying out of the necessary realism of our made-up pictures, we feel confident that we have only recorded, as far as distribution at least, the impressions of the moment. And in such a matter as this I feel quite sure that for all of you who may be passionately fond of realism, who may delight in the thing as it is, who may avoid too much thought, for fear of endangering what you think is not thought, but impression, I may be suggesting a valuable caution.

Those of you who are as fond of the extraor-

dinary work of Menzel the German as I am ;
who, like myself for the last forty years or so,
have followed with sympathy this very modern
worker, may still have noticed how conventional,
how artificial, is, very often, the framing — if I
may so call it — of light and shade, or the arrangement of groups within which are included studies
that, seen at a proper distance, make the photograph look careless in observation. Evidently,
with such a man, this is the fragment of past
early education which he has carried all along,
which is not his own, which perhaps he may
not see.

In colour also there have been practices supposed to be principles, — practices which were
evidently based on the memory of some successful
momentary arrangement.

I do not know whether any one still remains
who learned the principle of what used to be
called *the brown tree ;* but those of us who have
known painters of the beginning of this century,
or of the end of the last, can remember that
there was a dictum of the studios which stood

in the way of newer attempts that now themselves seem conventional, — attempts at introducing the unbroken prevalence of tones like
the greys and greens of trees and herbage.
Therein, at one time, the connoisseur required
that some patch of brown, of warm colour, some
brown tree in a landscape, should restore the
balance — suggest what we can now understand
to have been some feeling for complementary
colour.

The composition of colour in painting is a
matter so important — I mean that scheme of
affecting the eye and the mind which has been
so beautifully used by great and little artists —
that I dare only refer to it. One side of the
question, however, has always struck me as unexplained, and that is that the succession, the
inheritance of such means has been with us in
the West always broken; while in the East the
tradition of the balances and adjustments of
colour seems to remain uninterrupted.

It is not that I cannot perceive the possible
influence of the struggle in the West between

that tendency which took form in the Greek
and the opposite tendency which seems to have
been the genius of the northern races. A certain
something came to bloom around the Mediterranean, rapidly, within a few lifetimes; and ever
since the world of the West has felt the power
more or less. The Greek moved in the moving
breath of the World. With him art was fluid;
but though his influence permeated the northern
world, always that world protested, returned to
something set as soon as possible, returned to
arbitrary, savage, symbolic formulating, to patterns instead of the reality, to what looks like
archaism. It is not strictly barbarism; it is a
holding-on to antique ways. The savage is conventional on principle, and often on religious principle. This opposition persisted, perhaps, far into
the Middle Ages, and the turn of mind which
I am considering on several sides to-day may
be an atavistic survival.

In certain great painters — I might say it
also of smaller ones, but I am thinking of
Titian, of Veronese, of Rubens, of Delacroix—

the arrangement of colour has a similar effect
in the painting to the arrangement of notes in
music ; it is an arrangement of voluntary repetition, of harmonizing which is not hidden behind
the apparent mere representation of the fact. All
the more, then, does it affect the mind, by suggesting, as music does, a certain direction of
our feelings. The turn which the artist wishes
us to give to the mood in which we shall look
upon his work, our indulgence in the feelings
of joy, of sorrow, of sadness, or of triumph, has
therefore been called, perhaps not inaptly, the
orchestration of colour. This is rare among painters of the moderns who may have every excuse
for not utilizing this tremendous force ; because
the faces, the sides of their interest in what they
represent, may be so wrapped up in the accidental
details of nature, in the chance happenings of light
and shade, of expression, of dramatic action, of
place, that these more arbitrary intentions might
count too much — count too much as they are able
to control them. I say able to control them, because, with most of the greater men, even of those

who have not visibly used this architectonic scheme, there is at least no contradiction to its principles, and very often a strong suggestion of their having been felt.

But why is it so extremely rare among architects, or among the artists of decoration, to whom especially these principles, even if only felt in the blindest way, have given, at certain times, a power of affecting the mind, which with the scale of their means is tremendous when compared with the smaller effects, that the weaker and smaller, though more intellectual, methods of painting and sculpture can merely hint at. In the past the architect has given a golden glow to the interior, to lift you up into the New Jerusalem; has made his walls sombre with black marble; has greyed them with stone that was neutral; has made his building clear-minded — if one may so say. And what shall we say of the whiter thing, which is intellectual when it emphasizes fine thought, commonplace and courteous when it is used for average expression? Now why do we use all these things haphazard to-day?

One man likes this, another that, as if he were some little lady anxious about being in the fashion, and willing to go even against her complexion, provided she do nothing that others do not do. And at length architecture, the means of largest importance that we can use, takes on a dress of triviality; like the madonnas of southern countries, dressed in paper and satin, with real costly diamonds, perhaps. But that is relatively excusable.

I was thinking, a moment ago, of the extreme dignity of architecture as illustrated by a saying of Delacroix, — that a great architect was rarer than rare, and consequently held the very highest rank as an artist; because he had to find beauty in what is most irrelevant, — usefulness.

These were not the sequences I was thinking of, however, when I left off speaking about the mechanical influence of ideas of composition. Our processes, the processes of modern painters, are complicated, both in observation and execution. You know that the modern painter, in the development of specialty, has long lost the clue

of his relations to decorative art, to work done
in large buildings for fixed places, which work is
to be lit as the walls happen to be lit, not to be
carried about from building to building or from
room to room, in a portable gilt frame. Among
the painters or designers who have tried to take
up this lost thread of connection with architecture,
there was for a time, there is still, a fear of
abandoning some clearly stated and commonplace
basis of arrangement ; for instance, a method of
putting something in the middle to emphasize
the feeling of a perpendicular, and then something
on each side to recall, perhaps, the case of dividing the remaining halves by some suggestion of
a diagonal: that is, the *pyramidal* composition
of the books and of the schoolboy in art. But
Raphael did it, — and so did Homer write in
hexameters. Which is the important thing, the
hexameter or the Homer ? It is just Raphael's
beautiful way of escaping the suggestion of
grammar which is his charm. What you feel,
as you look at his work, is the poetic feeling,
the splendour of movement of the limbs, and all

the freer composition which has covered the
original, simple programme.

To save his statement of such arrangements,
to keep their arbitrary nature, to prevent your
forgetting that he was a licensed grammarian,
who had passed examinations, the modern painter
or draughtsman was obliged to give to his figures,
and other objects represented, a greater stiffness
than he saw in nature, and thus another distortion
of memories became and is still a habit.   To
think only of just so much and no more, in looking at nature, then wilfully to remember some
ancient way of doing which seemed both imperfect
and abstract (and about that I shall have
something more to say), to continue artificially
these contradictory memories — for we cannot
fully control the memory of actual sight — this
became the mechanism.   Now, perhaps, of all
things it is most difficult not to remember; to
forget deliberately while one is receiving impressions.   Were I told that it is impossible, I
should not contradict.

And another difficulty came in the way: the

older methods and appearances of representation were all synthetic, not analytic; were all more or less in the manner of that fish outline which I spoke of as done by the savage, — all that he can do; not an elegant, civilized choice. This for both drawing, as we call it — that is to say, choice of synthetic outline — and also for modelling and for colouring. Consequently the modern æsthete usually produced an unthinkable equation. His figures looked like the sections of an architect's work; for had he not tried to believe in the possibility of a single outline? And his colours were *applications* upon that interior section.

Note that we have seen the same sad blunder in the bas-reliefs which are modelled upon the outline of a section.

I have quoted a criticism — a criticism by a child — of this modern method, in a paper published last July in *The Century Magazine*. It ran this way: "The light of truth fell upon the subject from the words of a child who had been listening to a talk in which I, and others wiser than myself, were trying to follow out certain boundaries which outlined true methods of decorative art, and which kept to the received instructions of abstention from this and that, of refraining from such and such a reality, of stiffening the flow of outline, of flattening the fulness of modelling, of turning our backs on light and shade; — of almost hating the face of nature; and we wondered that when our European exemplars of to-day had fulfilled every condition of conventionality, had carefully avoided the use of the full methods of art in the great specialties of painting and sculpture, their glorious work had less stuff to it than a Gothic floral ornament or a Japanese painted fan. 'Father,' said the child, 'are you not all making believe? Is the Japanese richness in their very flat work so different from what you can see in this sketch by my little brother? See how his tree looks as if it had light and shadow, and yet he has used no modelling. He has used only these markings of the tree and their variation of colour to do for both. He has left out nothing, and yet it is flat painting.' "

Nor have the great workmen of the past, even the Egyptian, the painters of the Greek vases, left out things. The draughtsman like Caran d' Ache, the caricaturist, solves the difficulty in the same way, by the most decided use of synthesis, by making his line again like that of the savage — by implying colour and form and modelling and perspective in his line. But this is a personal method, impossible to teach by analysis, or we should all study for it, and do it, too happy in getting to the end at once, which end is to express what you care for most by the simplest means that will avail *you* — your personality, your knowledge, your experience; whether you do it in work that takes years, or whether you do it, like Caran d'Ache, in the line of a few seconds.

In the division of our subject that we last dwelt on, we can discern the dangerous use of a merely analytic method in creative work. There is this danger, though none of us would like to avoid it, of much knowledge in certain matters which can be *used* in artistic representation, that they are assumed to be the *objects* of artistic representation.

The object of artistic representation is not your knowledge, but your way of using knowledge. Certain learnings of form, for instance, such as are possessed by the anatomist, have often been a something between the things we see and ourselves. And this difficulty is based on so honourable a prejudice that it is only when we have so mastered our knowledge, great or little, that in comparison with our great fund of ignorance it seems but a trifle, — when we again become ourselves, as it were, — that we can truly be free of it and use it.

Looking at the subject from another point of view, if we were perfectly honest and gave our knowledge pure and simple, and nothing more, as being perfectly honest, we should still be perfectly artistic. We should express ourselves in that direction. Who has ever felt distressed as an artist by anatomical plates which described anything that he wished to know? As long as everything about them was carried out for no other purpose than instruction of that one kind, has the most sensitive eye ever felt a want of taste

in them? Is anything more beautiful than the
drawings which accompany certain purely scientific books of botany — those in which nothing
but the idea of the plant, the leaf, the flower, is
expressed? The beautiful arrangement and composition involved in nature's constructions cannot
be more honestly suggested.

Now suppose that the professor of botany should
imagine that he has what the French call a charming talent for painting; for the representation of
light and air, for the finest variations of colour,
for all that is evanescent, fluctuating, irreducible
to a set of lectures in botany; and then that upon
these knowledges he places the *appearance* of
things which — and notice this with extreme care
— is, both in nature and in art, a statement that
we don't see everything that we know. Unless
our man is at least as good a painter as he is bot-
anist, — I had almost said a better, — there will be
a veil of misstatement of fact floating in front of
his record of knowledge.

Many a time, when looking from the sea into
the interior of some island of the South Seas, I

have tried to guess at, to analyze the plan of the mysterious intricacy of mountain-lines confused in the ancient volcano-centres around which the islands are built. With each motion of the ship or of the whale-boat, these lines played one into the other; edges of great slopes, smooth and green, or broken with precipice and wreathed in coloured mist, that trembled in the sunshine. What would I not have given to have their map clear in my head, like my friend the captain, or the engineer officer who accompanied me. And yet I said to myself: "My friend's knowledge of the geography (in fact, my own knowledge, if I had the map before my very eyes) would only be a help, and only a help to *me*. He could not paint this fluctuating scene, the light, the colour, all the things by which, through which, the scene was there."

This knowledge of a map would have been an abstraction, an idea perfectly well represented by the fact that I could have looked down on the black and white lines which made this image of an abstraction, all dotted with figures of heights, streaked with long Polynesian names, — Oropāā, Táutira, Tēvă, Porionûu, names full of historical and legendary association, — while the image that I saw before me blazing in the sunlight had no legendary meaning, had no heights marked upon it — was, conversely to the flattened map, more like a vast curtain of lit-up cloud hung between the sky and sea. Would the fact that I knew the height in numbers of feet of the great waterfall that crawled down the cliff, help me to give its many motions, or the glistening rainbow cloud that hid its path half down?

And do not let us forget what I put in as a sort of parenthesis, a few moments ago : in painting, in painting more especially than in drawing, but in drawing also, in every form more or less, in every form of art which represents any part of our record of sight, one of the most important elements is a record of our ignorance ; a statement that at a certain place our sight was confused, that one thing intervened to prevent our seeing another. It matters not whether that one thing be an actual object that I can take hold of, — a rock,

a tree, or a wall; or a mere veil of mist, a glanc-
ing of light, the interference of one shine of colour
with another, the fact that my eyes' range has
stopped at a certain distance, at a certain angle,
in the same way as the furthest range of a tele-
scope is still limited. Therefore, we painters represent, as I think I said before, not only what we
see, but what we do not see; without that involu-
tion there is no such thing as painting. I remember how a well-known oculist, who had little
experience with painters, tested the sight of a
patient who was an artist. He was surprised at
the artist's avoiding the traps that are laid to
detect defects in sight, and at the artist's power of
describing and analyzing what he saw, what he
thought he saw, and what he felt he saw indis-
tinctly or with uncertainty. Said the doctor, " I
have only two cases of eyes with worse defects
than yours, but I have never met any one who
seemed to see so correctly."

" That," answered the artist, " is my profession.
My profession is to see correctly."

It is this difficulty of the learned man that confuses the mind of the small child. He too staggers through the world, on his little legs, laden with the enormous responsibility of the knowledge he has acquired. Look at his drawing; he has got a face turned half away; he has put one eye in it, but he knows there is another. Where is he to put that eye — that extra eye? He has to get it in somehow or other; and he will put two on the same side of the face, rather than go against his knowledge; which, as you see, like all knowledge, is imperfect. Over and over again, the child worries about the representation of the windows on the other side of the house, about what is happening inside; and I have seen drawings in which a child, troubled by the fact of the two legs of a man, which legs are on either side of a horse, has made apparently his horse transparent, so that you can see the other leg. Otherwise, to him, it was a one-legged man.

There is, in that small compass, again the philosophy of all our systems of representation. You see the difficulty that the child has in separating his thinking from his sight. He has, perhaps, by the time that he begins to draw, a very keen, a very delicate sight. As long as the colours that he sees can be used for use, — for eating the fruit, we will say, for catching the bird, for knowing where the eggs are, — he makes no mistake ; though — if Mr. Gladstone will forgive me — he cannot name the colours which he uses any better than you or I, for the purposes just mentioned. It is only when he has to represent to himself the action of these colours upon himself, that, as we have seen, he becomes confused as to what is asked of him. I have known children quite unhappy at finding these difficulties, and relieved at having this weight of knowledge placed for them where it should belong. The child has explained to us this cause of error ; he can also show us again what we have been considering, — the main intention of the work of art. When before he knows how to write or draw, perhaps when he first makes marks on the paper, he hands you an unrelated scribble, and says, "Papa," or "Mamma, this is a letter to say that I love you," there is the work of art in its first intention. And so when later (if he have the tendency inherited from Heaven knows how far back, nor how near) he plunges rashly into drawing, like the savage, he often makes a synthesis before which many an artist will pause, in admiration at the number of impressions co-ordinated in some single line. He is really, at that moment, further advanced than when he becomes a student, and is obliged, by slow analysis, to separate all these impressions, to learn what they are the sign of; to accumulate notions of the different schemes of facts behind them; the botany, the geology, the anatomy that we artists never know enough of; to go through the never-ending accumulation of memories of the use of materials; the æsthetic systems into which he is forced; the contradictory admirations which entangle him; perhaps even such considerations as I am now obliging you to weigh. I have seen the process begin very early with children; I have now, in corners and tucked away, drawings by children which represent boats and ships moving with the wind, and seen in various perspectives; carried, also, by the motion of the waves; all with an impression of nature and a relative accuracy admirable both to the artist and to the man who knows about the sea and ships. Later, in the life of the same children, the drawings that I have no longer show the same ingenuous character. The ship is drawn in profile (in reality with a tendency to making a section); masts and yards and rigging are accurately outlined, as if the little draughtsman were counting them all over in his mind, and asking himself whether he remembered them all. The impression of art has disappeared; in the case of some children, never to return.

The artist can hope that in his fullest development he may become again as a child; and that as he looks, or we look, at his work, it may seem impossible to discriminate between what is the ingenuous statement of ignorance, and the consummate synthesis of knowledge; what is the frank and fresh record of a momentary impression, and what is the deliberate cumulative statement of choice.

I am coming to the end of my reading, the last one of this series. You see clearly now why

I can say so little in this short space of time. Any one of my pupils, if really he gave out what he had noticed, could give us much more than the details I deal out to you amount to. How much more then, I, older and having lived longer; and having longer memories of all I have learned and half forgotten, discarded, reserved, amended, apart from what I have believed that I saw myself!

So that I feel as if the very despair of the case would show us how I can only have pointed in many directions; as from the central milestone of Rome, the Roman ways passed into the entire world. For our subject is the mirroring of the world by the means of our art.

We have considered many directions, however. We have seen of what is composed our arsenal of means: our memories of sight acquired from others or made by ourselves.

We have seen, as students, how absurd it is to copy the memories of others so as to pass them off as our own; how profitable to copy them so as to learn from them and *purify* our own.

We have seen how it did not matter if we did copy — provided we did not copy the surface, which is the dress of another man.

Thus Donatello, who was a greater sculptor and artist than we are likely to be, and who is to-day nearer to our observations than ever, more fresh, more original than ever, studied and copied the antique. So Niccolō Pisano was awakened by copying the Roman Tombs. So Raphael, who appropriated all of antiquity that he could, who absorbed Perugino, who learned from Fra Bartolommeo, who imitated Michael Angelo. As Michael Angelo himself first imitated the antique. As Rubens, who never forgot the Italian, but to whom we refer as the type of a distinctly different national art. As the architect of the Renaissance, who thought that he was copying the classics.

I might have decided many things for you: I might have said that this work of art was right, and that another one was wrong; I might, as the Chinese philosopher phrased it, have divided by black and white, and hard and fast. As a general, I might have made war on an enemy's country, and spared none but my friends. I might perhaps have shown you more distinctly that a white thing is white, and that a black thing is black; nor do I object to doing so in a proper place and time; for of all things, what we begin to doubt of is the well-known; and we can never be too sure that twice one is two — but what is one and what is two? I prefer going through what we might see or what we have seen, in some sort of peregrination, hoping to find principles through some way of dividing what we have seen.

All that older men can give is advice, and it is only in details that their experience can serve and be carried over into the future.

Since our art is composed of memories and affected by them, so the memories of thought, outside of what directly affects your handiwork, will either elevate or degrade it. So obscure and unfathomable are our latent memories, which have accompanied our recording of nature, that we are unconscious ourselves of their preponderating influence with each of us individually.

We can discern occasionally in some work of art, if we happen to have a clue, how much its peculiar turn, its importance, may depend upon causes that are not apparently included in the statement of its form. Nature, as we said, is everything that is outside of us, and our views and feelings about her problems can be expressed even in the tracing of an outline: the subject, as it is called in catalogues of pictures, is merely the place where we express ourselves. Remember what I quoted from Michael Angelo's talk to Francis of Holland; remember how, in the designs of Michael Angelo, you feel that you are in presence of a most serious mind, occupied with the end of life. He himself has lifted the veil for us, in what he has recorded of this constant preoccupation. Dr. Bode, the Director of the Berlin Museums, was telling me, this autumn, of his constant sense of Millet's religious turn of mind in the noble drawings of plants and flowers, which hang with other more clearly stated expressions of moral attitude, in Mr. Quincy Shaw's wonderful collection.

Sometimes the presence of strong feeling or high thought behind the work of art is expressed in a sort of contradiction. It is sometimes the hidden cause of a subtle disturbing charm that appeals clearly only to the few, until its existence has been long recognized; though that very informing element has affected the looker-on without his separating it from the subject represented. As its absolute proof can rarely be given, except from some fixed knowledge, it must often be only a matter of divination or surmise. Not so long ago, I was speaking to an artist whose beautiful work is touched by a certain elegance which approaches sadness. We were admiring a beautiful female model; and as he described with the enthusiasm of the artist, some particular delicate sublety of form that he proposed to embody at some future day, I noticed an expression in his face which made me ask him, "What else are you thinking of?"

"Of the fact," he said, "that all this that I am doing and others are doing is but the labour of little insects,—little living points upon this small speck of dirt, rolling in illimitable space, which we call the earth, and which is destined to perish unperceived in the multitude of worlds."

Let us remember that among our ancestors were Socrates, the sculptor, and Euripides, the painter. Last week, as I looked over that collection of Hellenic paintings owned by Herr Graf, so many of them mere perfunctory tradework, but all full of meaning, for reasons of historical association as well as of their methods and technique, I pondered in divided reflection. Anything made, anything even influenced by that little race of artists, the Greeks, brings back our mind to its first legitimate, ever-continuing admiration; with them the floating Goddess of Chance took off her sandals and remained.

I was amused at recognizing, in the work of Alexandrian or Egyptian Greek, some traces of method not far removed from the system of touches which we analyzed in the work of Mr. Bonnat; marks and scratches painted in like memories of the tooling of a cestrum; as well as the manner in which the brush or the cestrum moved in the distemper and the wax, and gave the direction of modelling; just as it has always been with Western work, almost as it is to-day. Hardly a trace of the vase outlines remained; the so-called modern idea of painting by colour, not by line, was there implied: and again, there is nothing new. The cestrum moving in the wax was used there as Euripides, the poet, used it, after he had given up the career of the athlete and had not yet come to write the verses of which it was said that they were "sweet as honey and the song of the Sirens." And Pyrrho, the philosopher, had also been a painter before he followed Alexander into the far East, and returned with memories of the Eastern contempt for the vain shadows of this fleeting world.

He had met the philosophy of India, the thought of the East, and may perhaps have heard from the first Buddhists the doctrine which represents our life as one of constant illusion, in which nothing is safe to rest on, but the small momentary obligations imposed by our every-day relations, by pity towards others and the ties of daily duty.

He had lived not so many years before these paintings which I was looking at may have been painted, and he, too, had used the cestrum and the hot irons and the wax. I remembered also that returning with the treasure of a philosophy, to his native Elis, where he served as high-priest, he passed his life quietly and humbly, helping the sister with whom he lived in household work, carrying garden produce to market, and sweeping the house. So, too, in the books of an Eastern author, who may have lived in Pyrrho's day, a Chinese philosopher and pupil of Laotzu, I have read a story with a similar moral. It is the story of the pupil of some sage, who at length attains Wisdom and a full comprehension of the law of the universe, about which he had fretted for many a day, anxious and uncertain. Then, when he has attained, as the word is, he retires to live at home, in silence, in ordinary duties; sweeps the room and feeds the pigs, says the text,

as if they were human beings. I confess to the
extreme pleasure that I take in thus bringing the
East and the West together, in noting that this
lesson is as modern as any that I could learn;
that is to say, that there is little difference caused
by the delay of a few thousand years, and that
another colour of skin does not affect the general
law.

And so with us, pupils of wisdom, the attain-
ment of any clear and high view of our art;
the dwelling in regions of noble intention; the
consciousness of having powers above the common,
require all the more, as proofs of having attained,
that we should have care of small things; that
we should cook the meals and sweep the house.
It will be to us the proof of a sober certain
holding of the higher principles of art, that we
care for the small matters that allow us to express
greater ones. For us there can be no details that
are unimportant; there can be no art without
a craft. ("Il n'y a pas d'art sans métier.") Everything that gives us a better hold upon our humble
materials, upon our use of tools, will be of con-

stant interest. Our life as workmen will never be tedious; and we can take a childlike and healthy delight in our work and its success; our paints and their preparation, our brushes, our canvases, our papers and varnishes.

We shall be curious of all methods that can avail; underneaths and glazes, preparations and retouchings. And the experience of others in all such matters we shall seek out and respect. We cannot tell how important the knowledge held by some older workman may be. And so, however full our philosophy or lofty our imagination, we shall still care for the washing of our brushes — for the sweeping of the house.

Have you not all been pleased as painters by the respect of the Dutch school for good work; for a sort of honesty and good faith in the very material offered? Can you not picture with approval, even though you may smile, the Dutch painter of high finish, whose room is as cleanly and orderly as a laboratory when a test experiment is being tried; who abhors dust more than any housekeeper can abhor it; who steals

on tiptoe into his studio, and almost withholds
his breath from disturbing the air about his
canvas; whose paints, whose varnishes, are culled
from all that the world of experience can supply;
who never loses a moment, and yet works slowly;
whose steps from first to last are all measured
and thought out; and who may even have, outside of this well-applied use of time for art, some
other more commercial occupation? That man
can stand in any presence: before the greatest
of masters. Has he not testified that nothing
can be too precious to adorn an idea — that time
does not exist in the work of art?

For on one side our art is as humble as on
another side it is great; and in this we but
mirror again the world about us, whose great
and small are but expressions of momentary
relation, are but as plains and hills melting into
one another. Terms are not final; there is
nothing in all creation which is not great;
nothing which is not small. To carry out all
these great ideas, small means are necessary.
For this all men are not equally forceful, nor

can all men be equally narrowed into the projection of themselves through the obstacles that meet them in the realization of their ideas, and which to men of larger views, less obstinate, too sympathetic, might often mean opposing truths.

It is possible, then, and I am far from denying or doubting it, that the defeated in life are not the most to be pitied. If there is one thing more than another that we can learn from the ideas which we have contemplated, it is that all that is most important is our attitude of mind, and that time is of no consequence. When I talked of failures, of *carrières manquées*, when I deplored the destruction of such a great painting as Titian's "Peter Martyr," when I regretted that Lionardo, or whomsoever you wish to name, had not lived to carry out his famous work, my Buddhist friends in Japan were used to say that these interrupted influences had continued through other worlds, as they had continued for a time in this one; that the sum of what we had tried for here, or had done, was to be added to what other worlds might see us do. The fuel is consumed, but the fire may be transmitted, and we know not that it comes to an end.

I hope and believe that my talks can have done you, as my students, no harm, even if they have done you no great good.

Every time that I speak to you of what you may be doing at the moment, every time that I have the actual to touch, I feel surer than I can be in this process of analysis by language, of at least insinuating some knowledge of experience, some application of principles, and of not being led to add what you have no use for yet.

Children do not learn to speak because taught by professors of the art, doctors in language, but because they live among people who can themselves speak.

The means I may use, therefore, may not be the best; the reasoning may be more or less faulty. The whole point is this: have you perceived through my language some ideas that may help you; have you been able to look at

ideas already known to you in a newer and
fresher way, as we painters look at our pictures
in the glass to see them differently ?

"When the fish is caught, what the trap was
may be for the moment forgotten ; when the game
is caught, the snare may be forgotten.

When the idea is expressed, the language may
be ignored." "But when," thinks the artist, "shall
I find a man to put aside language, with whom I
may be able to converse ?   For perfect argument
does not express itself in words."

APPENDIX.

Notes and Memoranda of Lessons.

A YOUNG man brings me a painting which in his mind is a representation of an idea. It is "The Vengeance" or "The Triumph of Justice," or something of that sort. He explains to me what he means by the different actions, and all the symbolisms that he has within the action — even to the accident of his choosing the colours of the place, the scene, the figures and their drapery.

I understand it to a certain extent; but I assure him that it might be quite possible that a man should think, without being out, that Justice is not blue but red; and another man might think that both were wrong and that it was green.

From that I go on and state to him the main question, and that is that the plastic arts — architecture on its artistic side, painting, sculpture — are not the best forms for explanation and develop-

ment of a moral and metaphysical notion. From
their very constitution they represent, not the abstract world which we make, but the world as
it is, out of which we disengage, through morals
and metaphysics, certain ideas which live only
in the world of metaphysics and of morals; they
do not really live in the actual world as constituted by an impenetrable Providence. It is the
pride of morality —the pride of metaphysics
— to disengage these ideas we think written all
over everything, — in our lives, in the things we
suffer, and in the things we see.

There would be no difficulty (any more than
there is in recognizing the ordinary facts of living) with these deficiencies of the arts, were it not
for certain people who have not thought deeply on
the subject, though they may have thought very
deeply in metaphysics or in science or in morals.
Properly speaking, these deficiencies are the
honour of the arts, because they make really a
full picture of the world as it is, without prejudice. In them are gathered not only these abstract ideas that we distinguish and draw out, but

all the supplementary ideas, all the supplementary facts of this world; and none of us can tell how much weight the unimportant and the accidental may have — how necessary to the Providence of the world are the innumerable unexplainable conditions, — the small facts which seem to contradict, the great things that deny, and the useless, cumbersome filling in of the entire universe.

Hence, the Japanese — who looks at our work, and who in himself, with his Chinese studies, has developed the relations of what art should represent and can represent best — is troubled by our allegorical and metaphysical representations in art. He understands them as far as they make a beautiful brocade or a beautiful ornament, or are clothed in fine human form; but to him they are not thinkable. He cannot see why Liberty — an abstract idea — should hold a torch. An abstract idea holding a torch, and so lighting the world, is to him absurd. The figure is fine, let us say; as a figure holding a torch he doesn't object to it; but as an idea it is small — not great.

He, on the contrary, approaches the Greek, who considered that there were essences or beings who were properly in charge, and influentially powerful in the ordering of the world and in taking care of its many divisions, — divisions of thought; divisions of feeling; divisions of physical existence that he understands. My Japanese friend understands Minerva; he understands the gods of his own religion; he understands our saints — our mediæval feeling for the saints; but he cannot understand the abstract representation of the kingdom of science or of moral quality.

*　　*　　*　　*　　*　　*　　*

Memorandum of lesson to Miss ——.

This point to note: in a composition in which the cadence of a number of movements ends suddenly with a return of line upon itself, the sensation will be of an accumulation of movement at the end which will prevent this end being quiet or in repose, even if intended to be so.

In a subject of pure composition in which the story is told by the arrangement of lines and figures, and by the truth of their motions, the background must necessarily be very carefully studied, as the least thing may throw the main lines off the equilibrium. Hence, naturally, the artificiality of backgrounds, — hence often their comparative unimportance, — meaning by that absence of detail, so as to reach the same end as a very successfully arranged composition of background, based on realities. Hence again the undesirability of introducing, as in one of the subjects criticised, an accidental naturalistic distance of trees and rocks, such as a Central Park landscape, not only because its accidental lines may clash, but because in its very essence of having no excuse for itself, except that it was true, it clashes with the whole idea of the figure composition, which has no pretence to having really happened; on the contrary, insists upon its being a well-selected artifice.

Our imitative means are so limited that we not only cannot weaken them, but are obliged

to reinforce them. Hence, for instance, in painting, the wisdom of reinforcing the sentiment of
the picture by its general impression of colour
or of light and dark. Hence the musical accompaniment of a song being in the direction of the
meaning of the words.

This is true in art — in nature, it happens
rarely. Whatever our own feelings may be,
whatever tragedy we may be suffering from,
even if it afflicted the entire human race without exception, the sky above might be more
smiling even than usual, and no actual picture
of the scene would give any idea of what it
really meant. It is only by art that these contradictions are disentangled.

If on the stage reality were represented, the
voice of the actor in its most agonizing moments,
in the tenderest passages, should be interrupted,
should be wiped out by accidental noises, themselves just as necessary as his — such as, we
would say, the passing of omnibuses, the creak-
ing of doors, the talk of indifferent people.

Hence in your composition of Narcissus, his

being in an open field, in midday, with the
nymphs coming up to him, is so much against
the mystery of his retiring within himself to
admire himself.

Your figure, which rests, does not rest *long*
enough. In the story it is a sort of contemplation, — at any rate, a looking-down into water
as a mirror, — and cannot be a momentary, quick
recognition, such as we get from a looking-glass
which makes a perfect reflection, and which we
are sure to get again easily.

In the South Seas, the girls ponder very long
over their reflections in the moving mirror, which
is all they have.

The same objection might apply in your composition of the judgment of Paris, where all the
figures stand in too open a pasture; that is to
say, too open as you have represented it, because
it is more natural than the figures, and I am
obliged to accept it as it is painted.

Apart from the story as it is given us, it seems
unreasonable, at least in fairy-land, that these
goddesses should expose themselves to be seen

by any accidental passer-by who crosses those
meadows that I feel are behind the trees. And
if you tell me that they can appear and disappear
at will, then I must feel that also in their make,
— their looks.

In the old story, Homer, who knew them very
well, seems to imply that they took great care
of their dresses and adornments; in fact, that
they were very much like ourselves, only a great
deal more so.

As to the studies from nature : you are making
a study out of your window on this very grey,
rainy, monotonous-looking day, and as I sit down,
taking your place by the window, I am not at
first struck by the fact that your grey sky is too
monotonous, more so than the brick wall which
you are also copying. You have transferred to
the brick wall the sense of colour that it gives
you, and you have given to the sky the dreari-
ness that one may feel by being rained on; but
now, as I sit here a little bit longer, I notice
that the real sky is full of innumerable movements — movements of shade, of form, of colour,

of light, of transparency, many more million
varieties than in all the many-coloured bricks
of that wall. I own that one does not notice
it at first, and that it seems difficult to prove
when one looks at that big, wet sheet of cloud
seen through the panes. But then what makes
it so living, and the wall so dead?

Why, simply that there is such infinite detail
flooded in light that you cannot quite detect it.

See, through the rain we at length notice two
clouds of the sky moving past. They have been
there all the time, but have come nearer to us,
and at length we see them. I mean that we
now see what their shape really is, — but we
have seen them all the time; and now that
we recognize them, we can discern the existence
of many, many others far back towards the horizon. These last are hidden by the rain, or vapour
further back in the distance, and behind them,
made indistinct by vapour, spreads higher up a
great mass of cloud. In front of everything is
a veil of rain and vapour. So that this apparently dull, flat surface of sky is in reality ex-

tremely modelled and complicated. In fact, if you will reflect a moment, there is more modelling in the sky than there can be in all the rest of the things you are painting,—that brick wall, the old chimney, and the roof-tops.

You see that they all look from where we are perpendicular, if I may so say, compared to the sky, which curves over and which is staged back, below, in infinite gradations.

Now you will see why so many paintings of the modern school make the sky look like a veil hung behind the landscape, as if the sky were on the same plane as the sides of the buildings that rise into it, and it had no other extension.

If you go up to the Museum, you will see why the skies of Corot look like skies; you will see why the skies of the good Dutch painters curve over and are wrapped around the landscape, so that you see the clouds hang over you.

The sky is *a place in which* the picture is. It is not something behind the picture. The fact that all these transitions and modellings are very delicate, far from the eye, usually not modelled by light and dark, but by transitions of colour, is what makes them difficult to render.

You will again recognize in the Corots these variations of colour in what are called his greys, which his imitators render by some kind of mixture of black and white.

The sky that we are now looking at is not only modelled by what we call light and shade, so delicate that we find it difficult to trace, but it is modelled by varieties of colour.

As you will see, towards the horizon, I mean our horizon, because the tops of the houses are over our horizon, it is a little yellower. The clouds that float in it, of which we mainly see the shadows, are more violet; the upper sky, where the clouds are thinner, is greener, meaning that there is the faintest suggestion of blue, and, if you will watch a little, you will notice that all this mass of low cloud where it is thicker and makes shadows as it comes nearer to the brick buildings, seems to harmonize with them and you feel that there is a little pink or rosy hue, more or less everywhere.

Were the sky to appear suddenly, you might see these fog-clouds — those that are low down, at least, look reddish. But as you have no contrast to help you, your eye is not very sensitive to this. Only if you do not feel it, and give some suggestion of it, you keep wondering why your painted sky is so cold and tea-boardy. For notice again, that properly there is more colour in this grey sky, dull as it is, than in the red brick wall against it.

This is the way you can detect it. Give me your palette. As you have it arranged, you have yellows and greens over to one side, and on the extreme other side you have violets and blues. In the centre you have dull reds and browns. Now as I mix the paints, you will notice that the sky tones are made from the fullest extremes, — the light yellows and pinks mixed with the violets and blues. It is true that they are blended, and make what we call greys.

But the brick wall is represented by a very small space of colour on your palette. Let us say a couple of octaves, the distance between the others being enormous. You will see, therefore, that it is merely a dulness of vision that prevents our recognizing this extraordinary wealth of colour in the grey. And now I wish to speak to you about something which I will take up at odd moments later.

Do not confuse paint and colour. Strictly considered, all these colours on your palette, and any combination you wish to make of them, are varieties of any one colour in the key of which you wish to paint.

Your palette can be looked at as a variety of blues, or a variety of reds. It is in the tone that you assume your painting in, that you will find the harmony of all these pigments. Should you, for instance, paint a large mass of any one pigment on your canvas without reference to any reality, and then insist that everything you paint from your palette shall be in harmony with that mass, and then you wipe it out, its influence will have coloured every stitch of paint or so-called colour that you have put in your painting. The result will be coloured, no matter how few the pigments you have used.

Theme — upon studies from the nude.

Necessity of a greater synthesis for the division
of light and shade so as to make the general construction appear more evident, as it is with figures
at a distance.

Answer to a question in lesson to Miss ——.

So you will teach me the tricks of the trade?
Yes and no. My special point is to make you
distinguish what is a trick of the trade, and what
is a principle of art, especially the art of painting.
That is the result that one comes to from the
comparative study of many works of art, such as
is afforded by museums.

Many artists and almost all young ones confuse
the means and the end. It is perhaps impossible
that that should not be, as the great point of the
worker in art is that execution should become
almost instinctive with him; nor can he be easily
a thinker.

I think that I am unnecessarily taxed by those
I am teaching by having to explain to them the

use, advantages or disadvantages of ordinary materials, — brushes, canvases, oils, mediums, etc. All these they ought to work up without me, and I can give them my experience, and that of others, about it. If we consider it from a serious point of view, as would be required from such a course as this, it might take at least a couple of hundred lectures, so that it must practically lie out of our scheme except as helping to explain occasionally, and ease the difficulties of a student. For example, there have been painters — modern painters — to whom the use of bitumen was so important as a help that without understanding this fact and its connections, we have no adequate explanation of their paintings, and of how they came to see bitumen in nature because it was convenient. Just as to-day a great many people see white lead, which does not exist in the atmosphere, any more than bitumen. Remember and remember again, and whenever you are in doubt, remember that pigments are not colours, nor light, nor air, nor shade, nor distance, nor atmosphere.

Remark to another pupil in connection with this.

Pupil. "I can't help painting very white—
and the flowers look very white to me. I don't
see how they can be whiter. But I think the
frame doesn't suit. It leaves the picture flat and
the flowers don't go back."

Answer. "Let me see the frame off from the
picture. Now please notice that when I put it
in front of the flowers which you are copying,
they seem to keep their place just the same and
do not stick out of the frame. I think it safer
to assume that the picture is wrong and the
white lead also. In fact, it is because they are
white-lead colour and not white-flower colour,
which is a very different thing, that they refuse
to take their place behind the frame."